THE LIKEABILITY FACTOR

Also by Tim Sanders

Love Is the Killer App

THE
LIKE
ABILITY
FACTOR

HOW TO BOOST YOUR L-FACTOR
&
ACHIEVE YOUR LIFE'S DREAMS

TIM SANDERS

Crown Publishers • New York

Library of Congress Cataloging-in-Publication Data
Sanders, Tim, 1961–
The likeability factor : how to boost your L-factor and achieve
your life's dreams / Tim Sanders.–1st ed.
1. Charisma (Personality trait) I. Title.
BF698.35.C45S26 2005
158.2–dc22   2004016875

Printed in the United States of America

Design by Robert Bull

www. crownpublishing.com

ISBN 1-4000-8049-5

10   9   8   7   6   5   4   3   2

First Edition

To my wife, Jacqueline. You are my muse,
my stronghold, and my partner in life.

Contents

| CONTENTS |

Author's Note

As part of the research methodology process for this book, I hired Zoomerang/Market Tools, a leading provider of research subjects and technology support, to recruit a wide sample of participants for a likeability survey. These prospective subjects were asked to fill out the survey and told they might also be asked to participate in follow-up e-mails and/or telephone interviews.

We eventually selected and spoke with more than a hundred people, mostly via phone, although several dozen interviews were conducted face-to-face. Each session lasted from thirty minutes to three hours. For this book, interviewees' names and some details about them have been changed to protect their privacy.

Stories told to me by attendees at likeability seminars I have given over the last two years in the United States, Italy, and Norway are also included in these pages. I elicited this information by providing seminar attendees with my e-mail address and a request to follow up with questions, comments, or suggestions, to which hundreds did. A number of these seminar attendees' stories are found in the book; again, names and details have been altered in the spirit of confidentiality.

THE LIKEABILITY FACTOR

Introduction

In the spring of 2002 Don Anthony, known as the don of morning-show radio disc jockeys, asked me to give a speech at an annual boot-camp conference for deejays. The topic: "How to Get People to Like You."

Don came up with the idea because, he explained, morning-show personalities aren't always likeable people off the air. Their fans may love them, but their coworkers don't. They have a tendency to burn bridges with their sales and production staffs and to fight with their station managers. Such behavior is generally written off as prima-donna star syndrome, but Don thought that for many of these deejays it had the potential to become a huge liability.

The subject interested me so much that I immediately rolled up my sleeves and dug into the assignment. What an interesting audience to address!

As for any new presentation, I planned to do as much research as possible. Don had given me a list of people I could interview, so I picked up the phone and got to work.

One of my first conversations was with a radio personality

named Jimbo, with whom the subject of likeability immediately resonated. Our long talk soon shifted from his radio audience to his concern about just one person—his morning-show partner, Michael Diamond.

Michael's real name is Mikey Wills, but when he became a shock jock he selected "Michael" as his professional on-air name because he figured no one would be afraid of a guy named Mikey. He added the "Diamond" because it sounded good, and soon enough Michael Diamond was a well-known, on-air schmuck.

He quickly became effective in his new, unlikeable role. He learned how to insult anyone on any topic. He figured out how to push people's buttons in the meanest way possible. He was willing to say anything to keep the audience's attention. Just as quickly, his show experienced phenomenal ratings and even managed to become syndicated in a handful of major markets.

Not everything went smoothly, however. Despite his becoming successful, no one *liked* Mikey anymore—except his listeners, and after two years even they seemed to be cooling off.

Meanwhile Mikey was having trouble at home. His kids were constantly fighting with him, and his wife, with whom he had entered a nonstop, no-holds-barred battle, was threatening to leave him.

In talking about his friend, Jimbo added, "Remember the television program *Married . . . with Children*? Well, if you can imagine it, Mikey's like an Al Bundy gone bad."

Nevertheless, Jimbo wanted to help Mikey, because the two had grown up together. From grammar school through high school, Jimbo recalled that Mikey had been one of the most popular people around.

"Mikey was the class clown," Jimbo said, "but he was also the human crying towel—I've never met anybody more sympathetic to his friends, whether it was the guy that lost the championship track meet or the girl who got a C when she expected an A. There was something special about Mikey, and everyone knew it. A special light just seemed to shine right out of his being."

Mikey's popularity continued in college, where he was elected president of his fraternity. But five years into his radio career as Michael Diamond, two things had happened. He'd become very successful, and he'd become a thoroughly unpleasant person.

A few weeks later I gave my talk to a hotel conference room jam-packed with morning-show personalities. They were a formidable crowd, sitting with their arms crossed in folding chairs, daring me to distinguish myself from the typical motivational speaker. Half of them looked as though they had spent most of the previous night partying, while the other half glared irritably with the resentment of people whose AA sponsor wouldn't let them go out.

The speech went over well. For the most popular part, I addressed a disturbing trend: increasingly, radio stations were willing to fire their deejays and replace them with a syndicated satellite feed. This feed was cheaper and easier because it meant no staff to worry about.

In contrast to this depressing news, I also mentioned studies showing that the more well liked you are, the more likely you are to keep your job. I could tell from the audience reaction—some gasped, some began talking with their neighbors, some squeaked as they moved uncomfortably in their chairs—that this was the most riveting piece of information I had delivered.

After my speech, I met Jimbo in person. Standing next to him, staring at his shoes like a sinner in church, was his partner,

Michael Diamond. Mikey knew what people thought of him, and why. As we talked, he glanced furtively from side to side, as if fearful that one of his colleagues would see him talking to me and yell, "Hey, Tim, don't waste your time talking to that jerk."

The scene reminded me of evangelist Jonathan Edwards's landmark 1741 sermon, "Sinners in the Hands of an Angry God." Edwards described a lake of fire that roared directly underneath us all, with only a thin and rotting layer of canvas constituting the sole bridge across that lake. That layer of canvas was God's forbearance, and it was wearing very thin. The congregation members hearing these words were so convinced of their doom that instead of walking to the altar, they crawled cautiously on their hands and knees, their faces as ashen as Mikey's was today.

Still staring at his shoes, Mikey asked if we could talk for a few minutes before the next event, so we sat down in a nearby lounge. There he told me that he knew Jimbo had revealed his recent personal problems, but rather than being angry about it, he was grateful. Mikey realized he was a man in crisis, and he quickly confirmed everything that Jimbo had told me.

He said he felt as if he were careening toward a Guinness world record for Most Hated Man—not something he wanted inscribed on his coffee cup.

"Your speech really got to me," he admitted. "I've become unlikeable. The only people left in my life are my listeners, and there's less of them now than ever before. My family life is on the road to becoming a family death. If I don't fix my personality defect, I'm going to be lonely for the rest of my life. Can you help me be more likeable?"

The man was sincere; the tears dirtying his cheeks were

proof positive that he wasn't happy with himself. I promised to help.

I asked him to give me some more time to think about his issues. He sent me some information about himself, including his publicity photo, which captured him scowling at the camera, and a personal note from his brother-in-law, warning that he needed to "find the real Mikey who my sister fell in love with or disappear from view–and leave the kids behind, too."

For a few weeks I let our conversation roll around in my head. I called him once and noticed that his voice-mail recording sounded hostile. It made me feel afraid even to leave a message.

In the meantime I sat down and reread Dale Carnegie's *How to Win Friends and Influence People*. I did a few more phone interviews with radio-station managers and executives to deepen my context. And I conducted some basic research on highly likeable people and their habits.

When I finally spoke to Mikey again, I gave him four pieces of advice on being likeable.

First, I said: "Check yourself. Have you listened to the message on your answering machine? Have you looked at your own promotional picture? Are you able to step outside your body and listen to the tone of your voice when you talk to your wife, your kids, or the staff at the station? In other words, can you be more *friendly* to the people around you?"

Next I told him, "Try to matter to other people–be *relevant.*" Mikey never bothered to learn about other people's wants and needs. "You've perverted John F. Kennedy's famous words," I explained. "You don't care about what you can do for others, only what they can do for you."

As a result, Mikey had basically made himself irrelevant to everyone around him. Why talk to Mikey, when you knew that nothing good would come of it? Besides, he was a terrible listener, often finishing other people's sentences because he was in such a hurry to bring the conversation back to himself.

My third piece of advice was "Develop your *empathy*. If you want people to like you again, you're going to have to take an interest in their feelings. I heard how important that was to you when you were younger. I bet you did it by being able to get under your friends' skins and into their hearts and souls. Once, you knew what it felt like to be someone else. It's time to go back. Do it again."

Then I paraphrased Dale Carnegie: " 'You will win more friends in the next two months developing a sincere interest in two people than you will ever win in the next two years trying to get two people interested in you.' "

My final piece of advice was "Get *real*." I told Mikey to ask his wife why she'd fallen in love with him, and to ask Jimbo why he still liked Mikey so much. I challenged him to find out what was truly likeable about his personality, and then to bask in it. "Likeability doesn't work if you have to pretend," I said. "Everyone is likeable. But people can tell the difference between sincerity and insincerity. Be the best Mikey you can be."

Down deep, I told him, you will find the Mikey that everyone is searching for. Once you prove that you're not faking friendliness, relevance, or empathy, once you prove that you can be a friend for real, you'll be amazed at the difference it can make.

A few months later Jimbo called me with an update. Michael Diamond was acting like Mikey again. He was also working on a format change for the show, switching over from nasty shock jock to compelling current-events guy. "It's great to have Mikey back," Jimbo said.

He added, "This is like a coming-of-age story in reverse. It's as if he's regressing back to his younger days when he was a better person."

Jimbo also said that Mikey and his wife had patched things up, and that Mikey was even getting along with his kids. They hadn't been to the radio station in years, but Mikey was now bringing them in for visits.

Fortunately for Mikey's career, the station's bosses had decided to drop the syndicated satellite feed idea, so Mikey and Jimbo were staying on as morning deejays.

The last thing Jimbo told me was "Everybody who deals with Mikey on a day-to-day basis is happy as heck that he's likeable again."

| | |

It was exactly when the phone call with Jimbo ended that I decided to write this book. I realized that likeability is truly the secret of a charmed, happy, and profitable life. And I knew that someone had to evangelize the importance of being likeable.

Yup—I'd gotten bitten by the likeability bug. That one exchange had rocked me, and I wanted to explore the subject further. Couldn't learning how to be more likeable change our world—and that of everyone around us?

More important, someone had to deliver the news that being unlikeable is a form of social cancer. A guy like Michael Diamond would wither like an unwatered plant if he continued down his displeasing path.

Nor is it healthy for the rest of us to be around these people.

One of the more stressful parts of modern life is dealing with all the unlikeable people who populate it. If they don't kill themselves with their own unpleasantness and rudeness, they'll drive the rest of us to drink.

Our nation is so focused on efficiency and productivity that we forget that likeability is truly our lifeline. People who are likeable, or who have what I call a high *L-factor,* tend to land jobs more easily, find friends more quickly, and have happier relationships.

People who are unlikeable, or who have a low L-factor, generally suffer from high job, friend, and spouse turnover.

I now believe that having a high L-factor isn't just a way to improve your life, it's a way to save it.

After my speech to the deejays, dozens of e-mails started pouring into my in-box—all told, more than thirty radio personalities contacted me with anecdotes about the impact of likeability. They told me stories about themselves, their on-air partners, their families, and their friends. They talked about job opportunities squandered, marriages dissolved, relationships lost. Just like Mikey, all of them wanted to know: What was this thing called likeability—and how could they get it?

I began to see that for many, the question "What is your L-factor?" prompted the response "Frightfully low." And as I talked more about likeability and asked, "How is your life going?" those with a low L-factor would reply, "My life is fraught with disappointment and frustration."

Surprisingly, once I'd decided to read every book on the subject, I found that there weren't many. Yes, there were a few books on how to make two people like you in sixty seconds, or how to make sixty people like you in two seconds. But I couldn't find one that explained what likeability looks like in the world and how it operates.

I wanted to create a construct that could teach someone how to establish and maintain long-term likeability. To do that, I started ingesting all the information I could find on the topic. My nights and weekends became Internet surfing sessions on the L-factor.

Almost immediately I found huge collections of research on the subject in two fields: advertising and politics. The former showed that highly likeable advertising was most effective in selling products of all varieties. The latter, consisting of thousands of studies dissecting dozens of elections, found likeability to be one of the major factors in deciding the winners.

Even just while watching television, I saw the effects of likeability in play. I was particularly impressed with a recent documentary that showed how John F. Kennedy's likeability (and his opponent Richard Nixon's unlikeability) influenced their famous 1960 presidential debate. And on the popular television talent competition *American Idol*, I witnessed likeability elevate an overweight twenty-four-year-old contestant named Ruben Studdard from talented unknown to beloved winner.

In the meantime I was also haunting Stanford University's library system, rummaging through its stacks and databases, locating academic studies that demonstrated both the effects of likeability and proven techniques and disciplines to achieve it. I soon came to realize that university psychology departments around the world have been quietly studying the science of likeability for decades, and over the next six months I filled several filing cabinets with studies both strange and sane, from an article in Australia's *Journal of Psychology* on the impact of beards on perceived likeability to a University of Toronto study on the relationship of court settlements to the plaintiff's personality.

All in all, it became clear that unlikeable characteristics are a primary reason for failure, whereas improvements in likeability offer excellent explanations for breakthrough successes. I'd never seen any statement of crisis so firmly supported by clinical research, yet so hidden from ordinary view.

Everyone I met, from lawyers and executives to techies and teachers, had seen and felt these truths, but none could articulate them. So I became an immediate receptacle for their horror stories about the unlikeable people who were driving them crazy as well as the likeable folks who seemed never to lose, whatever the odds.

My curiosity about likeability became an obsession, and my obsession led me to accumulate thousands of pages on the topic. Eventually a pattern emerged, something profound yet simple. I found similarities in everything I read, a virtual consensus on the path to unlikeability—and the path to recovery.

Because I was obsessed, I soon made likeability the preferred topic for my speeches. Across the country and the world I went, armed with my research and hypotheses. And everywhere I traveled, there was more to learn. One audience member at a talk I gave pointed out that his likeable wife always got better service than he did, whether at a restaurant or in the doctor's office. That observation lead me to excellent research on the subject.

Another time a seminar attendee discussed his grandfather, who'd lived a long and resilient life due in part to a large circle of friends. Soon I'd added the relationship of likeability to health to my research agenda.

Still another attendee shared how his boss had confided that his attractive personality had given this man an edge when it came to surviving company-wide layoffs. Until then I'd only seen the L-factor as a way to land a job rather than a way to keep one.

Ultimately I realized that all of us are somewhat likeable, but if we're able to make ourselves more so, if we're able to raise our L-factor by even just one or two points, life will feel better—in any or all of the ways already mentioned, and in others I haven't yet discovered.

If you raise your L-factor, you will harness one of life's most powerful forces. You will see it everywhere you go, and you will wonder why you never thought about it before. You will discover that nothing feels better, and is better for everyone around you, than achieving the highest L-factor possible.

Part One

THE L-FACTOR

1

LIKEABILITY

If you're like most people, you're neither at the top nor the bottom of the likeability scale. If you were at the top, you'd know it, because your many friends would constantly tell you what a charmed life you lead—and you'd have to agree. You can imagine what this life might look like: You'd still have your share of bad news and bad luck, but it would seem as if all of life's close calls fell firmly in your favor.

But what would life look like if you were at the low end of the likeability scale? Probably something like this:

You wake up, roll out of bed, shower, dress, and leave for your job. On the way you have an eight thirty appointment with your internist, Dr. Smith. Dr. Smith is, as always, overbooked and harried. You sit in her waiting room for what seems like an eternity, yet you know that only one patient was scheduled before you. You're angry because Dr. Smith always seems to give other people a great deal of time, and in fact, when the patient emerges, you see that he and the doctor enjoy a solid rapport—they're chatting amiably, exchanging restaurant recommendations, and Dr. Smith is promising to call him later that day.

You, on the other hand, snapped at Dr. Smith during your last visit because you were so angry that it took so long to see her. Now you do it again, and after a brief and unpleasant appointment, you're out of the office with a quick diagnosis and an absentminded promise to call you sometime in the future. (1)

You drive off to work. Already upset, you're dreading the day's first appointment, which is with your assistant. Your company's direct competitor, the Widget Corporation, has been on a hiring binge. Both your assistant and your coworker's have been offered jobs with better salaries at Widget's headquarters. Yesterday you found out that your coworker's assistant has decided to stay, because the two of them are truly bonded—the assistant loves her boss and knows he'll try as hard as possible to match Widget's offer.

You're hoping your assistant will make the same decision because he is industrious and effective and you don't have time to train someone new. Unfortunately, he tells you that he is taking the Widget offer after all. You wonder if the fact that you humiliated him in front of his peers last week has anything to do with it, but you doubt it—he deserved to be dressed down. You sigh and comment about how hard it is to find a loyal secretary. For the umpteenth (and last) time, he reminds you that he is not a secretary. "Whatever," you mutter. (2)

Your mood increasingly foul, you now march off to your late-morning meeting. Here you find that your client has given you low marks in your annual account performance review. You can't believe it—you think he's scum, and the idea that he thinks the same of you is shocking. The world is so unfair. And it seems more unfair when your boss tells you that there isn't enough money in her budget for the raise you were expecting. (3)

The rest of the day is unpleasant. Ever since you happened to mention to that horrible assistant in legal that she could lose a few pounds, she seems to have had it in for you, and you can't get your contracts back from her office in a timely fashion. Whatever happened to professionalism? you wonder. (4)

But you really crash when your insurance agent calls to let you know that the settlement from your recent car accident will be less than you'd hoped. The hearing was as contentious as you'd expected, but now you wonder whether you lost points with the judge by suggesting she return to law school for a refresher course. Why is it that so few people can take constructive criticism? (5)

When you arrive home that night, you change and go off to your son's Little League game. You had been expecting to win the election for his team's coach, but a new boy's father got the nod instead. How unfair, you think. No one has been asking for the job more loudly, or pointing out the faults of the other fathers more succinctly, than you. Even so, this new guy, who barely seems to know anything about baseball (as you have often mentioned), is very popular. You hate guys like that. (6)

That night you get home a little late. You decide to grab a beer from the refrigerator before going to bed, and there you see a note from your wife. On it she has written that she's so unhappy in the marriage that before she goes through with her divorce threats, she wants you both to see a marriage counselor. She's already set up a meeting. (7)

Finally, you climb into bed and think back on your miserable day. What is it about other people that makes them so difficult? Wouldn't life be so much better without them?

Now, let's review your day through the prism of studies revealing why it went the way it did.

1. Doctors give more time to patients they like and less to those they don't. According to a 1984 University of California study: "A physician attribution survey was administered to 93 physicians. [They] also viewed videotapes demonstrating patients with three combinations of likeability and competence. There were significant differences in treatment, depending on the characteristics of the patient: The likeable and competent . . . patients would be encouraged significantly more often to telephone and to return more frequently for follow-up than would the unlikeable competent or likeable incompetent [patients]. The staff would educate the likeable patients significantly more often than they would the unlikeable patients."

2. In his book *Primal Leadership,* author Daniel Goleman studied the management habits and business operations of several hundred major companies and found that a positively charged work environment produces superior profits via reduced turnover and increased customer satisfaction.

3. A Columbia University study by Melinda Tamkins shows that success in the workplace is guaranteed not by what or whom you know but by your popularity. In her study, Tamkins found that "popular workers were seen as trustworthy, motivated, serious, decisive and hardworking and were recommended for fast-track promotion and generous pay increases. Their less-liked colleagues were perceived as arrogant, conniving and manipulative. Pay rises and promotions were ruled out regardless of their academic background or professional qualifications."

4. A 2000 study by Yale University and the Center for Socialization and Development–Berlin concluded that "people, unlike animals, gain success not by being aggressive but by being nice.

The research found that the most successful leaders, from CEOs to PTA presidents, all treated their subordinates with respect and made genuine attempts to be liked. Their approach garnered support and led to greater success."

5. In 1977 author Dulin Kelly wrote in the court preparation trade publication *Voir Dire:* "One item that keeps reappearing in cases tried or settled, is the likeability factor. If your client is a likeable person, this characteristic will in all likelihood affect the outcome of your case in two ways: First, the jury will want to award compensation to your client, because the jurors like him or her. This may overcome a case of close liability. Second, there is no question that if the jury likes your client the amount of compensation is likely to be higher."

6. In *You've Got to Be Believed to Be Heard,* author Bert Decker points out that George Gallup has conducted a personality factor poll prior to every presidential election since 1960. Only one of three factors—issues, party affiliation, and likeability—has been a consistent prognosticator of the final election result: likeability.

7. In 1992 Dr. Phillip Noll of the University of Toronto surveyed a representative sample of fifty married and divorced couples and concluded that one of the primary elements of marital success is likeability. Easygoing, likeable people have one-half the divorce rate of the general population. When both parties are congenial, the risk of divorce is reduced by an additional 50 percent.

Likeability is more than important, it's more than practical, it's more than appealing. Likeability may well be the deciding factor in every competition you'll ever enter.

People believe what they like. People surround themselves with friends they like. People want to envelop themselves in others' likeability.

Every person alive has an L-factor, which is the indicator of how likeable you are. Every one of us is either likeable or unlikeable.

For simplicity's sake, I have created a likeability scale ranging from one to ten: on this scale, one represents very unlikeable, while ten represents very likeable. The average rating is a five. At the lowest end of the scale, a one denotes the most unlikeable person imaginable. Hitler, Darth Vader, and Jack the Ripper come to mind. On the other hand, at the highest end of the scale, a ten represents the most likeable people in the world; Abraham Lincoln and Peter Pan are probably tens.

In general, if your L-factor is three or below, you need vast improvement. Four to six is average, while seven and above is good. Few people actually attain a ten.

Keep in mind that most people's L-factors are not constant; they vary dramatically at different points in their lives. Harry Truman was not universally admired during his tenure as president, but after much reassessment he is now seen as an immensely skilled leader, resulting in an L-factor that has soared from a mid-level four to a high nine; Ebenezer Scrooge from Dickens's *A Christmas Carol* went from a one to a ten after just one night of ghostly visitations.

Still, your L-factor permeates all aspects of your life. A low L-factor makes itself apparent when doors slam in your face, when you can't find a partner, when your doctor rushes you out of her office. A high L-factor shows up when you have more than one job offer, when your kids want to spend more time with you, when the court awards you that extra bit of money.

Likeability itself is a difficult term to define. Dictionary definitions can be as vague as "easy to like," "attractive," or "appealing." But after researching the worlds of psychology, physiology, and personality, I define it thus: Likeability is an ability to create positive attitudes in other people through the delivery of emotional and physical benefits.

Someone who is likeable can give you a sense of joy, happiness, relaxation, or rejuvenation. He or she can bring you relief from depression, anxiety, or boredom.

By being likeable, by generating positive feelings in others, you gain as well. The quality of your life and the strength of your relationships are the product of a choice—but not necessarily *your* choice.

After all, if everything were a matter of choice, you'd select the best job, the best mate, and the best life in the world.

Your life is really determined by *other people's* choices. Do you want the job? It's up to the woman doing the hiring. Do you want to watch football all day on Sunday *and* stay happily married? It's up to your spouse or partner. Do you want the jury to find you guilty or innocent? It's their choice.

The more likeable you are, the more likely you are to be on the receiving end of a positive choice from which you can profit.

We'll talk more later about how choice works, but in the meantime, remember that the best choice you can make right now is to boost your L-factor and become more likeable. Not that you're not likeable now, but all of us can become even more likeable if we apply ourselves to the task.

A young man named Mohan came to my company, Yahoo!, in 1999, just before the entire Internet industry took a hit. Since his arrival, many layoffs have occurred, as well as a number of reorganizations and downsizings. Yet Mohan, with no seniority, has managed to stay employed throughout it all, even though he's held four different jobs.

Why?

Because Mohan is so well liked. When push came to shove—and many people were indeed pushed or shoved out—boss after boss stood up for Mohan, trying to find him a new place in the organization. Three powerful managers who usually don't decide on low-level hirings became personally involved. Mohan wasn't necessarily brighter or more competent than the others who were let go. He is indeed good at what he does, but he is so personally appealing that his presence makes the workplace more pleasant.

As the above illustrates, the L-factor's importance in our professional life appears when choices are made about who is going to get hired or fired, or who gets the raise. We are constantly making choices at work, and when things are close, we go with the person with the highest L-factor.

If you're the boss, the L-factor becomes relevant when you must decide who's going to get that special project that will mean spending extra time together. You want to surround yourself with talented people, but when two people are equally talented, you'll pick the one you like better.

If you're an employee, the L-factor comes into play when your boss asks for more than is normally required, and you go that extra mile because you want him or her to succeed because you like him or her so much.

Job candidates are more successful if they're likeable. They're more likely to get second interviews, and more likely to get short-listed for jobs. They are also more likely to keep their jobs, both in bad times and good.

A few years ago the market research company Booth Research released the findings from a study organized by the out-placement firm Challenger, Gray & Christmas involving thousands of people who had recently been discharged or downsized. The study concluded that the decision regarding who stays and who goes in a downsizing boils down to the L-factor: how well people are liked by their supervisor. Company president James Challenger sums it up: "People who are not liked by someone in authority are always the first to go when business conditions become unfavorable. It's not just enough to do a good job. You have to find ways to increase your likeability factors in the eyes of your employer."

It's one thing for a guy like Mohan to keep his job during tough times. But what about reaching your potential in your career? Likeability can play a huge role in that aspect of your professional life as well. According to the 2000 Yale University study mentioned earlier, "most successful leaders, from CEOs to PTA presidents, all treated their subordinates with respect and made genuine attempts to be liked. Their approach garnered support and led to greater success."

| | |

Likeability is equally important in your personal life, where it can be the glue that holds a relationship together through thick and thin. No matter what you're dealing with, a likeable personality can help, or even solve, problems.

My good friend Sarah, for example, has faced several considerable challenges. She has suffered from a chronically bad back and also struggled with alcoholism for several years. She and her husband, George, have faced many financial difficulties, and once they even lost their home. A salesperson, Sarah must travel constantly for her job, often spending weeks at a time away from her family.

Yet Sarah's marriage is relatively happy and her friends and family, including her two rebellious teenage daughters, all adore her. Why? Because Sarah is so likeable. George worked hard to help her through whatever problems arose, from alcoholism to bankruptcy. Similarly, her friends and family rooted for her whenever she slumped, and they were always around to provide much-needed support, both emotional and financial. Cheering rather than jeering, they liked Sarah enough to see past her momentary problems and knew that with a little help she could recover from whatever life threw at her. And so far she has.

You'll recall that research shows that likeable people have stronger marriages. But it's not just Sarah's marriage that helps her—all her relationships do. A study of 174 women conducted by Sheryl Aronson, a relationship therapist and a codirector of the Institute for Relationship Assessment and Development in southern California, found that women who described themselves as friendly and likeable received a number of benefits. "Such women were more likely than others to be in love [and] to have had more love relationships. . . . These women and their positive self-concept gave them a greater capacity for love and romance. Their relationships are not only more sexually intimate, but seem to be more intimate on emotional levels, as well."

Whether you are involved romantically, socially, or as a

friend, you need likeability to be successful in your relationship. Psychotherapist and author Terry Real observes that "unlikeability exhibits the absence of sensitivity and care. People attempting to sustain close relationships while behaving in unlikeable ways are like people hoping to have an automobile last over 100,000 miles without replacing the oil in the engine."

Sarah's personality has many appealing features, but not the least of them is her likeability, which drives what seems to be her eternal happiness.

2

UNLIKEABILITY DOESN'T WORK

Thomas Alva Edison once declared, "Opportunity is missed by most people because it is dressed in overalls and looks like work."

Being liked requires work. Just about everyone is likeable to someone, but few of us are as likeable as possible to everyone (or at least, to everyone whom we'd like to find us likeable). Most of us need a makeover in our personal tendencies and reaction habits. A high L-factor is a form of social fitness, and achieving it can be just as tough and time-consuming as developing physical fitness.

Yes, for some, likeability comes naturally. But such people are very rare, and even they can improve their L-factor. I've always believed that you can become twice as good at something you are already good at faster than you can cut a weakness in half. In other words, it's easier to grow the talents you possess— you have momentum!

Yet there are many people who don't believe in developing likeability, who don't want to change. They think that likeability is a sign of weakness.

The problem is, unlikeability doesn't work.

One reason is that the 2000s are not the 1950s. Welcome to the new world of abundance. I've always joked that the letters in Yahoo! really stand for You Always Have Other Options—because we all enjoy many more choices than our grandparents did. We have more choices of where to eat, whom to marry, where to work, whom to hire, and so on.

In the past, we had excuses to explain away bad marriages and terrible jobs: "I can't afford to," "I have no other option," "I don't know of any other job," "I have no way of meeting other people." All of these were reasonable twentieth-century statements.

Today, however, options abound. Technology has made communication so easy that the world is now a global marketplace, no matter where you live. For example, the Internet provides new paths for those who've been coping with too many low L-factor people at work—just by turning on your computer, you can visit one of many job-posting Web sites that provide thousands of employment opportunities. Or you can send your résumé out to a group of friends who can then forward it to thousands of potential new employers. The possibilities are only as old as the Internet itself and are increasing every year.

In the movie *Jerry Maguire,* fired sports agent Maguire prepares to form his own company so he can do things his own way. He then says openly to his old office workers, "Who's coming with me?" His assistant meekly replies, "I'm three months away from the pay increase, Jerry. I have to, uh . . . you know, stay." In other words, even the assistants now have options they once may not have enjoyed.

It has certainly been my experience that when vendors are

surrounded by a multitude of competitors, they have to be nicer. They're more likeable. They put in that little bit of extra work.

Take this test: Walk into a local coffee shop that's within a stone's throw of a Starbucks, and I bet you'll find some very agreeable counter people—because they're all too aware that you could walk next door. As Jeff Taylor, the owner of PT's Café in Topeka, Kansas, told me, "Without the love, it's just coffee."

Similarly, in the past, you may have had what I call a situational friend—someone who seemed to represent your sole option for socializing in a particular situation. Maybe he or she was your only friend at work, or your only neighbor, or the only person you had time to see in your personal life. And in those situations you put up with the fact that he or she was often in a bad mood, or insensitive to your feelings. You had no other options. But now if you want to make a new friend, you can go online to Friendster.com or to an AOL chat room. Or you can visit a site like Classmates.com and reconnect with an old friend.

People with options are empowered people, and empowered people demand a positive environment. They surround themselves with what they choose to buy and whom they choose to spend time with.

Here's another way to view it: There's too much information in today's world, and our defense mechanism to sort through it all is to vote with our gut, to go with what we feel. We look for shortcuts, and those shortcuts are called brands. The reason you buy Tide detergent at the grocery store is that you don't want to read fifty labels. You trust Tide because you already know it works.

This efficiency model has spread to our personal life, where we strive to build our brand. "I am a good boyfriend." "I am a good officemate." "I am a good member of my community."

These labels are all personal brands that show that you have developed trust with people and built a likeable brand.

In contrast, people with a negative reputation have few successful relationships. Think of the characters on the hit 1990s sitcom *Seinfeld*. Low L-factors kept all of them single for the show's entire run. George Costanza was neurotic beyond comprehension. He wore away at you until your teeth itched. Jerry Seinfeld was a perfectionist without sympathy for anyone else's flaws. Elaine was like a fabulous freight train of disaster. To know her was to realize you could live without her. And Kramer was simply insane. They were fun to watch, but you wouldn't want them in your life.

Besides the choice factor, here are four additional reasons why unlikeability is no longer an option.

1. *Short-term thinking is dying.* Short-term thinking is the belief that the moment is all that matters.

There was once a time when this kind of thinking was not only accepted but normal. A few decades ago we didn't yet believe we needed to consider the future. We weren't yet wired to understand that if we spilled chemicals into a river, the surrounding environment might be harmed; all that mattered was getting rid of our garbage. We didn't yet understand that screaming at our kids might result in negative consequences—all that mattered was shutting them up. We didn't yet know that eating staples such as white bread and white rice could lead to long-range health complications; we just wanted to wolf down a quick meal.

Today, like it or not, we've been forced to become long-term thinkers because it's necessary for survival. We know that our actions have consequences over time. Today's small, thoughtless act could result in tomorrow's disaster.

Being unlikeable is like expelling toxic waste into your social life. Insulting someone is like releasing poisonous chemicals into the air. Screaming at someone is like forcing them to ingest harmful pollutants. Yes, unlikeable behavior can produce a specific, desired result in the short term—when you shriek at someone, you might get what you want out of sheer fear. But if I'm aware that what I do to you today will make a huge—and negative—difference in how you feel about me tomorrow, I am much less likely to throw a verbal jab to get you to do my bidding right this second.

Psychological warfare won't work in the long run. It is much less likely than likeable behavior to produce positive results because it creates antagonism, resentment, and discontent.

As noted earlier, one of the hallmarks of the likeable personality is the ability to register another person's values and opinions. The long-term thinker requires this skill to predict the future successfully. We've all become emotional meteorologists when it comes to our personal and professional lives, thinking and worrying about what the future will hold for us.

As a culture, we are learning that we don't need a surgeon general's report to prove that unlikeable behavior trades a short-term benefit for a long-term problem. Our society now asks "what if" and looks one, five, or twenty years ahead to imagine future effects.

Similarly, people have become aware of the severe long-term consequences of negative behavior on their lives and those of others. This makes the unlikeable person of the past exactly that—of the past. The future is in likeability.

2. *Individualism is waning.* The concept of teams is on the rise in fields from sales to family counseling. These days the phrase "There is no *I* in the word *team*" is uttered not just in locker rooms but by psychologists and counselors in offices to help families patch together broken lives and revive faltering relationships.

Synergy occurs when two or more people produce more value together than they could produce individually; achieving it has become a quest for individuals, companies, and entire nations.

In his bestselling book *The 7 Habits of Highly Effective People,* Dr. Stephen Covey uses nature to illustrate the potential of synergy versus individual effort. "Synergy is everywhere in nature," he writes. "If you plant two plants close together, the roots commingle and improve the quality of the soil so that both plants will grow better than if they were separated. If you put two pieces of wood together, they will hold much more than the total of the weight held by each separately. The whole is greater than the sum of its parts. One plus one equals three or more."

To be synergistic requires that we become interdependent. Just a few people working together can create an organization with the power of hundreds. Here's an example: Not long ago some of my friends realized that each of them had been contributing money to fight AIDS. Instead of giving money individually, they decided to pool their resources and came up with an idea to auction off their professional services—one was an accountant, one a physical trainer, one a masseur, and so on. They managed to raise ten times the amount they would have given the charity if they had continued their separate efforts.

Interdependence isn't the same as dependence. Rather, it's a relationship in which, by relying on another, you become stronger. Interdependence is one of the goals of any great family, civic organization, or company.

It's hard to be interdependent and also be unlikeable. Certainly you can be independent and unlikeable, but you won't get as much done in this day and age. You may even be admired, but around you successful teams will thrive while you plod on, alone.

Simply put, unlikeable behavior produces a negative environment. In 1999 group communications consultants James Wallace Bishop and Dow Scott published a research paper in *Human Relations* magazine about the impact of unlikeable people and teams. They found that if a worker's job stress "causes her to become irritable and cranky with her coworkers, they may begin to view her as a difficult person who is unlikeable and unpleasant. Conflict is a short step beyond this personal dislike. If unhealthy conflict goes unresolved for too long, team members are likely to quit or search for alternatives."

Harmony, then, is key to any successful team. In 2002, after many years of research, *Investor's Business Daily* offered team leaders ten pieces of advice. At the top of their list: Always be positive—and beware of a negative environment.

For eons, unlikeable people, playing as loners, have managed to survive and thrive. Because they never had to cooperate or collaborate, their negative attitude was harmful only to themselves. But in today's world, where technology has made it possible to form teams for any activity from sports to social organizations, teams tend to win while single players tend to lose. And as the rise of teams continues, unlikeable loners will have to join larger groups or face extinction. The good news is that this may help convert more of the unlikeable into the likeable.

3. *Boundaries are dissolving.* At one time we all maintained distinct boundaries between our personal and professional lives.

Those boundaries let the monster of an attorney put on his coat at five o'clock, drive home, and be the loving father at the dinner table by seven.

Today at work we make personal plans on the Internet, while at home we log on to the computer to check our corporate e-mail. As the brick wall that once separated professional from personal crumbles, we are slowly becoming the same person 24/7. It's become much harder to pretend to be a good person at home when your neighbors can read about your reputation at work on the Internet.

According to the research company MetaFacts, more than 50 percent of the working population communicates with their family and friends from work via cell phones and e-mail or instant messaging. Of this same group, up to 75 percent log onto their work computer from home or while traveling. As Sonia Livingston, professor of social psychology at the London School of Economics and Political Science, says, "The Internet blurs those key social boundaries that once organized our physical spaces—intermingling work and home, learning and play, producing and consuming."

According to author Howard Rheingold in his 2003 book *Smart Mobs,* our grandparents were actually part-timers. People who grew up in the early part of the twentieth century worked an average of twenty to twenty-four hours a week in true nine-to-five jobs, with an hour off for lunch and two coffee breaks a day. That's unheard of in the modern economy, where the average person labors an average of fifty-eight hours a week, counting work done in the car, at the home office, and anywhere else our portable electronics take us.

Life can't be compartmentalized between "professional" and "personal" anymore. It's tough to flourish at home when you have to cope with the distractions of an unpleasant workplace. It's equally hard to succeed in your career if your unlikeability provides you with a miserable personal life and all the accompanying agitation.

Given these facts, the best solution for managing a boundaryless life is consistent living. At the end of the day, you're going to have to decide: Do I want to be a high L-factor person in all areas of my life?

The more you are required to live just one life, the more you will have to choose between unlikeability and likeability.

4. *Success has been redefined.* My grandmother, a product of the Great Depression, raised me to value a lifetime of financial security in which I would never lose my home and could afford to send my kids to college, drive a nice car, and enjoy an occasional steak. For the most part, financial security meant being able to maintain one's lifestyle without worrying about going broke.

Today our goal isn't financial security—we want financial freedom. Freedom from what? Freedom from facing ugly choices in life. Freedom from working on projects that make us feel sick. Most of all, freedom from working with people we hate.

A 2004 CNN survey found that only 43 percent of American workers are happy with their boss. In fact, the primary reason people say they started a business is that they hated feeling like a slave to a negative company environment or a negative boss.

According to Mark Foyer, producer of the cable television show *Financial Opportunity Spotlight,* "There are thousands upon thousands of Americans who save their money while working for an abusive boss or negative company so they can quit and open their own small business. They consider this not retirement, but a form of empowerment. At least one out of three people who watched my show every week works for someone or some company that they can't stand and they are planning their escape."

Financial freedom doesn't mean not working. It means having a job we enjoy, coworkers we like, and a pleasant environment within which to work.

A positive workplace is so important that most people would make a financial sacrifice to achieve it. An April 2002 poll of thousands of working and nonworking individuals conducted by the job-seekers' Web site Monster.com found that 73 percent of respondents said they would accept less money if they could be happier at work.

Executives are realizing this. A November 2003 survey by the research firm Robert Half International found that "one third of all executives surveyed have changed their opinions in the last few years, and now say that the work environment is the most critical factor in keeping an employee satisfied in today's business world."

The relationship between a positive work environment and success is well rendered in the 1980 comedy *Nine to Five*. Mr. Hart, an old-school executive, runs his division of a faceless conglomerate with arrogance, distance, and unfriendliness, creating a thoroughly unlikeable corporate culture. But everything changes after three female employees kidnap him and tie him up in a leather harness for six weeks. With Hart gone, his three abductors reorganize the workplace in a more positive style, adding day care, job rotation, and a more supportive office atmosphere. Productivity as well as profits quickly soar. The chairman of the company's board, noticing these changes, adopts them company-wide and transfers the hapless Hart to the South American jungle.

Today success is as much about quality of life as it is about quantity of material objects. Increasingly, people are concerned more with their daily environment than with money or power. Unlikeable people are finding that their money purchases them little when it comes to people—they can buy cars and helicopters, but they can't buy affection and loyalty. Their grip on our lives as despotic bosses, controlling spouses, and mean-spirited clients is slipping as our twenty-first-century society reexamines its fundamental goals and priorities.

Human relations consulting firm Towers Perrin's 2000 report suggests that this sentiment is widespread: "It appears that between 40 and 45 percent of the United States workforce in our sample is at risk right now, in danger of leaving for another job when the economy turns around and opportunities open again, or in the interim, just clocking time on the job, doing the minimum required."

The new success is about freedom, not simply security. Negative people will find it increasingly difficult to motivate workers, players, and teammates.

3

LIKEABILITY WORKS

Whenever I travel to Manhattan, I stay at the same hotel. I like the facilities and the familiarity: the doormen, the bellhops, and the desk clerks know me, and I have a good relationship with all of them.

One doorman, whom I call Gentleman Jim, asked me recently what my newest book was about. I told him, and he smiled as though the proverbial light had gone on in his head. He recalled the story of a customer who had screamed and ranted about how terrible his room was, and how he deserved something much better. Jim told the man that if he called the front desk and was pleasant, he would be surprised how helpful they might be. But if the guest continued to talk rudely, he'd probably find his towels weren't exchanged and his bed remained unchanged.

Jim said that he'd been trying to coach all his repeat guests in the art of likeability. "People are beat up in New York. Pleasantness is about the only good thing we get out of work. I will stand in the middle of the street and let a taxi run over me for a likeable person, but not for some bastard who growls at me and then thinks he can buy my loyalty with a three-dollar tip."

Likeability makes things happen, not just while staying at a hotel but throughout your entire stay on this earth. Following are likeability's most important consequences.

LIKEABLE PEOPLE BRING OUT THE BEST IN OTHERS

The other day I was in a sporting goods store with a short-tempered friend. As usual, it took him only a few minutes to become irritable when he couldn't find the warm-up suit he wanted, and he took his frustration out on the salesman who'd been doing his best to help.

When my friend finally asked if someone could check the stock at the store's other branches, the salesman told him that it would take a day to get that information. Clearly, it would actually only take one phone call. But the salesman had no intention of going out of his way to help my friend, who stalked out of the store in anger, muttering how no one understood good service anymore.

I couldn't help but notice that other customers in the store were being graciously assisted. The fact is, some people simply receive better service than others. And I don't just mean at stores and restaurants but also at the post office and the bank, at doctors' and lawyers' offices, at school and at work.

The reason? Likeable people inspire others to give more.

In a 2002 study by the National Service Foundation, more than four thousand people were asked about their perceived levels of service throughout their lives. They then answered questions whose answers indicated which of several personality types they fell into. The survey showed that the "likeable and competent" customer was three times more likely to have a positive service experience than the unlikeable customer.

One place where the kind of service you receive matters a great deal is the doctor's office. Here numerous studies have shown that likeable patients bring out the best in their physicians.

Barbara Gerbert, a professor of behavioral sciences at the University of California at Berkeley, conducted a study administered to ninety-three physicians, measuring their level of service to different types of patients. Gerbert found that "there were significant differences in the treatment dimensions, depending on the characteristics of the patient. . . . For example, the likeable and competent patient would be encouraged significantly more often to telephone the doctor and to return more frequently for follow-up than would be the unlikeable patient."

Perhaps you don't care about the service you receive from your own doctor, but if you have children, you surely worry about their care. In a survey of twenty-five hospital doctors initiated by Roy Meadow, a pediatrician at St. James's University Hospital in Leeds, England, researchers studied what happens when both likeable and unlikeable parents bring in children. Not unsurprisingly, children with likeable parents received better health care and were more likely to receive follow-up appointments.

Furthermore, the amount of time the doctor spent with the family at clinics was longer when the patient's parents were likeable. Likeable parents seemed to draw out more time, attention, and conscientious behavior from physicians and health-care workers alike.

Likeability brings out the best in people throughout life. For example, likeable teachers often become positive influences on their students. In the 1980s Drs. Seymour Uranowitz and Ken Doyle at the University of Michigan conducted a study entitled "Being Liked and Teaching: The Effects of Personal Likeability," in which they surveyed thousands of students and teachers over a four-year period. They concluded that "students who perceive a more positive student-professor relationship and like their professors may be more motivated to learn because the presence of the professor is rewarding to them, and they care more about obtaining the approval of the professor."

Another, more recent study by researchers at the Family Development Center, in conjunction with the University of Minnesota, concluded that "students become better learners when they experience warmth and friendliness, when they receive praise, recognition, and respect."

Similar studies show similar results in professional situations. Leadership is enhanced by the likeable personality type. William Heyman, CEO of Heyman Associates, a leading executive search firm, spent three years measuring the essence of leadership against personality traits. He determined that "a real leader understands two important issues: one, having the energy to share the experience shoulder-to-shoulder with staff; and, two, that sensitivity on how to be a good coach leads to the perception of warmth and openness and what I call 'likeability.'"

Heyman states that a leader's success is measured in part by how well he or she gets along with others; he notes that employees will take on more burdensome and undesirable tasks for managers with likeability.

Think about your own experiences with coaches, bosses, parents, and teachers throughout your life. Try to recall exactly what moment inspired you to raise your bar and give a little more. Most likely you'll remember it was a likeable person who most inspired you.

Here's an example from American history. Former president Dwight Eisenhower was known as one of this country's most inspiring leaders. You may recall him as the "Ike" of the 1952 campaign slogan "I like Ike." Particularly relevant to this discussion was Ike's ability to inspire his troops. Alistair Horne, author of several books on World War II and a wartime veteran who knew Ike personally, believed that Ike's likeability was the source of his leadership.

Says Horne, "Eisenhower . . . was a great man, loved by his associates and perhaps uniquely fitted for the role of supreme commander of the huge allied forces. I remember well, when I was a wartime soldier, the powerful boost in morale that his broad can-do smile and that fresh confidence imparted to the troops who were about to embark on the most terrifying experience of their lives on D-Day. Ike's extraordinary ascent was due to a combination of qualities, but mostly his efficiency and his sheer likeability. He even caught the eyes of top soldiers like MacArthur, Marshall, and Patton, who were to become his willing subordinates."

Likeability gets results, from the general store to the general practitioner to the general himself. Wherever you are and whatever you do, you'll get the best out of others when you present your most likeable self front and center. You really do catch more flies with honey.

LIKEABLE PEOPLE GET RECOGNIZED

Have you ever wondered why some people seem to garner all the praise and glory, while others are overlooked? Do you think it's just because some people are lucky enough to be in the right place at the right time? Or is it because they work so much harder than others?

The fact is, all of us want to be recognized and praised. Charles Taylor, author of "The Politics of Recognition," asserts, "Due recognition is not just a courtesy we owe people, but a vital human need."

Whether we're students or workers, fathers or mothers, we all strive to be acknowledged for our efforts. And research shows that your likeability will have a tremendous influence on your capacity to garner that respect and recognition.

One unexpected area in which recognition rewards the likeable is parenthood. If you have children, you know how much you want them to appreciate the good job you've done raising them. In 2000 the Foundation for Childhood Development and Parenting conducted a survey in twelve school districts and found that "children with . . . likeable and involved parents were eight times more likely to nominate their parents as World's Greatest Mom or Dad than children with neutral, inconsistent, or unlikeable parents. They go beyond simply acknowledging the support and shelter their parents provide and instead show deep appreciation."

Dr. Vera Rabie-Azoori has worked in family mediation with a variety of hospitals throughout North America. In a 2000 interview on *WebMD Live,* he discussed his work observing children vying for attention from their parents or guardians.

Children diverge into distinct personality types, he said; among these distinctions is likeability—one type of child is seen as more likeable to the parents, the other as less easy to like. In general, not only is the former type favored, but the additional attention and affection tend to nurture a more relaxed personality in these favorite children, who in turn become even more likeable, not only to their parents but to their peers as well. While most parents insist they don't show favoritism, they frequently do, and it is their high L-factor children who end up getting the extra attention.

Likeability is also rewarded with recognition in the classroom. I'm fond of using the example of teachers to illustrate likeability because teaching and learning provide an excellent metaphor for how we lead much of our lives. Almost everyone we meet has the ability to teach us, whether it's a parent, mentor, business associate, or friend. And your ratings as a teacher will be driven by your likeability.

The University of Hawaii's Michael Delucchi conducted an extensive survey of student course evaluations to investigate the link between liking and learning. Delucchi found that "students who rate their instructor high in likeability reward that instructor with high ratings on overall teaching ability. . . . Likeability was the strongest predictor of students' overall ratings of their teachers; and, as a predictor of ratings, likeability had three times the effect of perceived learning."

Not only do likeable teachers receive recognition in the form of better ratings, so do likeable students. Tyler Fisher, an English major at the University of Central Florida, dreamed of becoming the first UCF student to win a prestigious Rhodes scholarship. (Each year universities submit approximately fifteen hundred applications for the Rhodes; thirty-two students actually win.)

Against long odds he succeeded. Why? Many on the UCF campus say it was due to his ability to win friends and fans, a trait obvious throughout the entire competition. Tyler had the same excellent grades and test scores as his competitors from fancier schools. But in the end, because they liked him, the judges found a way to award the first Rhodes scholarship in the history of UCF to Tyler.

Michael Mcleod, a staff writer for the *Orlando Sentinel,* spent a day with Tyler during the heat of the scholarship competition and noted that although he looked like the kind of student who would blend in unnoticed on campus, his likeability always shone through. McLeod wrote that Tyler "is recognized and greeted every few moments, by professors . . . and by other students."

On the job, your likeable personality can have an equally positive influence on your annual review, that piece of paper you receive every 365 days judging you as outstanding, mediocre, or below expectations. Cindy Ventrice, author of *Make Their Day! Employee Recognition That Works* and owner of the consulting company Potential, Unlimited, observes, "Bosses are emotional people, just like everyone else. A likeable employee that produces positive feelings in others, including their manager, will get better annual reviews and job performance marks than an unlikeable employee. And more importantly, the likeable employee gets more feedback throughout the year, allowing for continual improvement."

In a follow-up telephone interview, Ventrice told me that managers fear unlikeable employees and their toxic reactions to any type of feedback. She added, "Ongoing feedback from managers is critical to perceived excellence and career potential. If your only feedback is annual, and it says you meet expectations, you don't feel appreciated or in line for a promotion."

This vital need to be recognized may be more controllable than you think. Your personality will have as much to do with your recognition as your results or even your luck. From the classroom to the living room to the boardroom, when you are likeable, you are praised. You are acknowledged. And you know that feels great.

LIKEABLE PEOPLE OUTPERFORM

One period of our lives when superior results are demanded of us is, strangely enough, childhood. Despite being young, we are expected to achieve good grades, stay out of trouble, make friends at school, do well on tests, perform chores at home, and so on. It's not easy.

The good news is that being likeable can help a child perform better. Likeable children enjoy many advantages, including the ability to cope more easily with the stresses of social interaction and growing up.

In her book *Understanding Child Stress,* Dr. Carolyn Leonard states that children who are likeable, optimistic, and personable fare well and are able to gain support from others. This leads to resilience and focus; a child who has adequate emotional armor can continue down the path to success. Much research shows that resilience, the ability to recover from or adjust early to misfortune or sustained life stress, has enabled children to succeed in school, avoid drug abuse, and develop a healthy self-concept.

Why does a likeable child more easily navigate stress and do better in his or her life? Because likeability helps create what's known as a positive feedback loop. The positive feelings you invoke in other people are returned to you, creating constant encouragement and an antidote to the daily strains of life.

This feedback loop continues into adulthood. To return once again to the example of teaching, learning becomes easier with a likeable personality. Michael Delucchi of the University of Hawaii reviewed dozens of studies to determine if likeable teachers received good ratings because of their likeability or because they in fact taught well. Delucchi found that "students who perceive a teacher as likeable, in contrast to those who do not, may be more attentive to the information that the teacher delivers, and they'll work harder on assignments, and they'll be more receptive to grading, and they will learn more."

You may have noticed this pattern in your own life when you try to give someone advice. The more positive your relationship with that person, the more he or she seems to listen, and the more you feel certain that that person has heard you and intends to act on your words.

Communication through likeability has also been studied and modeled in the workplace, particularly in the field of productivity improvement. A 2003 study by researchers at the University of Michigan found that "friendly and positive employees are more productive because they possess greater communication capabilities."

Likeable and friendly people engage more deeply in conversations around projects and tasks, and people pay more attention to them, developing leadership as well as eliminating misunderstanding. Misunderstandings can be the heart of unproductive activity at work.

Jeffrey Sanchez-Burks, the lead psychologist on the Michigan project, stated: "A personal unlikeable style tends to restrict the bandwidth of information the person attends to in the workplace. And this creates a miscommunication, like ships passing in the night."

Whether dealing with a project or a plan, the likeable manager tends to be skilled at accomplishing one of the job's most critical components: convincing others to act and helping them to understand exactly what the manager wants them to do.

This process has a powerful impact on a company's potential success. Robert Levering, the primary researcher for *Fortune* magazine's "Best Companies to Work For" studies, found that "organizations with positive employee relationships produce 15 to 25 percent more productivity. And the reason is that managers have that connection with their employees, enjoy loyalty from their employees. The employees look for solutions, and they don't need to be micromanaged because they want to see the manager succeed."

If you stop to think about the greatest work you've ever done, you'll probably realize you didn't do it for yourself; you did it for that likeable boss or some other favorite leader. Inspiration is at the core of productivity. It's an emotional reaction that's been shown to enhance the overall benchmark of a great company: profits.

As a follow-up to his bestselling book *Emotional Intelligence,* Daniel Goleman studied the management habits and business operations of several hundred major companies. In *Primal Leadership,* Goleman reported that a positively charged work environment produces superior profits via reduced turnover and increased customer satisfaction.

Be it on the factory floor or in the executive suite, performance improves in the positive environment created by the presence of a likeable personality. People respond with loyalty and that extra bit of effort. Not only do likeable people get the job done, they motivate others to get the same results.

LIKEABLE PEOPLE OVERCOME LIFE'S CHALLENGES

Whoever you are and whatever you want, challenges will always stand between you and your goals. No one—no matter how likeable, lucky, or wealthy—can avoid weekly, if not daily, trials that require marshaling all the necessary skills needed to triumph.

Talent, brains, and money can all be keys to winning these challenges. So is likeability.

Consider life's trials—literally. Today's atmosphere is litigious; a 1999 National Center for State Courts survey showed that 27.9 percent of respondents had been either a defendant or plaintiff in a civil or criminal court. And according to a January 2000 Roper Starch survey, at least 13 percent of Americans have filed a lawsuit. The odds aren't bad that you too will someday go to court.

Miami jury consultant Amy Singer has worked with clients for almost twenty years. Her advice: "For defendants, likeability is the number-one factor. It's basic psychology. Why? Because you don't want to believe someone you like could do something bad."

Take the case of physicians, who are often faced with medical malpractice suits—some justified, some not. Likeability can mean the difference between success and failure.

John Clifford, senior partner in the San Diego law firm

Drath, Clifford & Murphy and president of the San Diego Defense Lawyers Association, wrote a 2001 report for lawyers on
the issue of medical malpractice. He concluded: "In medical
malpractice suits, jurors' concerns regarding the physician are
focused almost exclusively upon his or her competence and likeability. Although jurors want to know the physician is well
schooled, what they most evaluate a physician on is his or her
likeability, their perception of that 'bedside manner.' "

Now, while you may not be a physician, and may be part of
the shrinking percentage of Americans who never appear in a
courtroom, you still face metaphorical trials all the time. And
often enough, you can win them with the aid of likeability.

For instance, millions of Americans suffer from disabilities
and disadvantages. Their personalities can make a tremendous
difference on their ability to succeed.

In 2002 the Hope Network, an agency that provides social services to thousands, issued guidelines on the topic of personality
and disabled and disadvantaged people. Among its conclusions:
"Our emphasis is on helping people, disadvantaged and disabled,
capitalize on their strengths and minimize barriers to employment. While their skills are essential to job success, so, too, is their
likeability. We encourage and motivate them to sell themselves
with enthusiasm, and consider this one of the most important
factors in their future employment."

Numerous training programs for those with a variety of disabilities also stress likeability. For example, the National Resource
Center on AD/HD (attention-deficit/hyperactivity disorder) produced a 2003 report called "Social Skills in Adults" that looked
at the challenges faced by AD/HD patients, as well as potential
solutions.

Their primary recommendation for coping with AD/HD was to "increase likeability. Many with AD/HD are considered to be high maintenance. Therefore it is helpful to see what they can bring to relationships to help balance the equation. Developing or improving any of the likeability characteristics (examples include friendly, unselfish, sincere, honest, and understanding) should help one's social standing in life with AD/HD."

The experiences of professionals who work with people with disabilities reinforce the above report. My friend Doug, a social worker in a depressed part of Appalachia, works with a blind quadriplegic woman named Virginia. Her patient and loving mother, Carole, has taken care of Virginia for years, but Carole is growing older and needs medical attention herself. What keeps this story from verging into complete tragedy is Virginia's extraordinary likeability.

Whereas many people with Virginia's challenges might be bitter or angry, Virginia is a delightful woman capable of charming anyone who visits her, from friends to inspectors doling out the state's few grants.

Virginia was recently one of several hundred people who applied for a rare grant that would allow her to continue living at home. After months of completing applications and undergoing interviews, Virginia received her money. Doug feels this happened because she is "so thoroughly likeable and lovely that people have an urge to help her. They want to find ways for her life to improve—and they do."

Besides having physical disadvantages, millions of Americans also face socioeconomic disadvantages. Many can't afford to attend college, yet they must compete in the working world against those with advanced degrees. Once again likeability can be the solution.

Barry Gilmore of the Social Data Research Corporation conducted a 2000–2002 study on the topic of undereducation and employment potential. He concluded: "Popular and positive-minded employees frequently transcend their socioeconomic backgrounds to achieve extraordinary career advancement. While it is difficult for a less educated individual to compete against others with advanced college degrees or a well-heeled set of contacts, it is possible through one's ability to socialize."

Consider the case of parents who face constant challenges due to their socioeconomic background. Whether it's a single dad raising children in the ghetto or a divorced mother of six struggling to feed her family, challenges must be overcome to make sure the children prosper. A 2001 study by the National Longitudinal Survey of Children and Youth that examined high-risk children found that likeable parents can have a tremendous impact on their success: "Many parents today feel overwhelmed by the task of raising their children in these high-risk situations and sometimes feel powerless in the face of the complexity of child rearing. However, we have discovered that children's social relationships are the outcome most affected by the parenting practices, specifically positive parenting. These factors include high praise, agreeableness, supportiveness, and positive interaction."

Through thousands of case studies, the survey determined that disadvantaged children of likeable parents can flourish as well as those with wealthy but unlikeable parents. "The size of the impact of positive parenting on the children's social development, especially for at-risk children, is noteworthy. It is so large that the mean score of children in at-risk families with positive parenting are exactly the same as those in non-risk situations without positive parenting."

While the complexity of challenges you face in life can be baffling, your likeability may get you through. One of the most inspiring stories about overcoming multiple challenges through likeability is that of Rudy Tomjanovich, known in Houston as lovable coach Rudy T. of the local professional basketball team, the Rockets.

Tomjanovich was born to an alcoholic shoemaker in Hamtramck, Michigan. His father, who wished his son would work rather than play sports, discouraged him from his love of basketball. There were no clinics or courts available, so young Tomjanovich practiced in the alley behind his home. And because he was skinny and awkward, his coaches told him to forget about playing high school basketball. But Tomjanovich was so popular with his teammates that they gave him a chance, first as equipment manager, then as a scrub player. He soon became a star on his high school team, won a scholarship to the University of Michigan, went on to set collegiate records, and in 1970 was selected as the number two pick in the NBA draft.

For six years Tomjanovich enjoyed great success with the Rockets. Then in 1977 he faced another challenge that nearly ended his life. When a fight broke out on court between Rocket Kevin Kunnert and Los Angeles Laker Kermit Washington, Tomjanovich ran over to stop it. Washington slammed him with a vicious punch to the face that sent him to the floor in a heap. It took three towels to clean up the blood.

According to *Sports Illustrated,* Tomjanovich suffered fractures of the face and skull, a broken nose, a separated upper jaw, a cerebral concussion, and severe lacerations, and was leaking spinal fluid into his mouth. The doctors compared his injuries to those suffered by someone "going through a windshield at 50 miles per hour."

Many people thought Tomjanovich wouldn't live through that night, while many more assumed he'd never play again. But after multiple surgeries, Tomjanovich returned to play a few more seasons, then retired at an early age.

But soon Tomjanovich's popularity afforded him another chance in the sport. He asked Rockets general manager Ray Patterson for a job; starting as a scout, he moved up the ranks to became the team's coach. In just three years he turned the losing Houston Rockets into a successful team that won back-to-back world championships.

One of the reasons Tomjanovich was so successful was his likeability. "Even though I had a lot of negativity in my life," Tomjanovich said of his fight to get his life back, "I wanted to do positive things for other people." And it worked. As coach, he was supported fully by his players, including star center Hakeem Olajuwon, who said, "He's been so enjoyable to play for. He doesn't have an ego."

Even after all his successes, Tomjanovich continued to face challenges. In the early 1990s he succumbed to alcoholism, and by the end of the decade he'd entered an Alcoholics Anonymous program. Yet the entire city of Houston rallied around him and upon his full recovery continued to support him as a coach until he stepped down to take a front office position in 2003.

Richard Justice, writing for the *Houston Chronicle,* covered Rudy for more than twenty years. He says, "We knew of his battles with demons such as exhaustion and alcohol and his seemingly constant struggle to accept life on its own uneven terms. . . . We knew he had a big heart. . . . We liked him."

The article was titled "Likability Rudy T's Legacy."

LIKEABLE PEOPLE ENJOY BETTER HEALTH

"An apple a day keeps the doctor away." That saying has been around for centuries. Now how about this one: "Being likeable every day keeps the doctor away."

One of the primary reasons likeable people often enjoy better health than the unlikeable is self-esteem.

In 1999 Mark Leary, a professor of psychology at Wake Forest University, wrote a paper titled "Making Sense of Self-Esteem." In it he said, "The attributes on which people's self-esteem are based are precisely the characteristics that determine the degree to which they're accepted by others. Specifically, high-trait self-esteem is associated with believing that one possesses socially desirable attributes such as personal likeability."

When we're likeable, we feel our likeability reciprocated, and that in turn increases our self-esteem.

One of the benefits of this process is that it helps us withstand stress. Stress can cause, among other ailments, increased heart rate, which over time can lead to anything from high blood pressure to heart failure. Brian Hughes, a researcher at the National University of Ireland in Galway, conducted a three-year survey of more than six thousand adults on the topic of heart rate and how they respond to stress.

His report shows the effectiveness of high self-esteem in overcoming physical ailments caused by or associated with stress: "Men who report low self-esteem over time exhibit elevated cardiovascular responses to stress. Specifically, in our study, the difference in elevations of heart rate during stress was exaggerated in low self-esteem participants, but indiscernible to the participants who had high self-esteem. In other words, sometimes our body does not react as negatively to stress; and, as a result, we avoid a lot of the self-destructive tendencies of a stressful lifestyle."

Harvard University's Dr. James Messina, author of the textbook series *The Tools for Coping,* says, "One of the negative side effects of low self-esteem is that its victims suffer high-stress illness like ulcers, colitis, high blood pressure, heart disease, and cancer." It's as if people with low self-esteem didn't have a buffer to let the stress pass through them without physical ramifications.

High self-esteem also seems to affect the immune system. Dr. Nathaniel Brandon is a Los Angeles–based psychotherapist and author of more than twenty books on the psychology of self-esteem. Self-esteem, he says, is "the immune system of your mind. A healthy immune system doesn't mean you won't become ill, but it reduces a susceptibility. The same is true psychologically. In my practice I have found that those with strong self-esteem have a resilience in the face of life's difficulties and ongoing stress."

Earlier in this section we established that likeable people are less likely to be divorced or alone and are more likely to have stronger social contacts. According to Richard Daft, a professor at the Owen Graduate School of Management at Vanderbilt University, "People high on the agreeableness scale (positive, good-natured, cooperative) tend to make friends easily, and they often have a larger number of friends than those low on agreeableness (negative, unfriendly, uncooperative) who have fewer close relationships in their life." The absence of friends can affect your immune system and even your ability to recover.

English psychologist Maureen Rice reviewed decades of literature on the science of popularity and health. Her conclusion: "The science of popularity is compelling. Significant research we've done shows that popular people . . . have stronger immune systems, fewer physical ailments, lower incidence of mental health problems, and they live longer than loners and introverts. Popularity, then, is literally a matter of life and death."

Perhaps likeability can be considered an ounce of prevention. In early 2004 researchers at Sahlgrenska University Hospital in Stockholm, Sweden, released a study concluding that men with the "most social support were about half as likely to develop heart disease as men who had the least social support."

This study tracked hundreds of men for fifteen years; according to study author Dr. Annika Rosengren, "These results likely apply to women as well, since previous research has shown that, among women with heart problems, those who have few quality friends they see on a regular basis tend to have more widespread disease than others."

Friends are an important antidote when you do become ill. Eugene Kennedy, a professor of psychology at Loyola University of Chicago, wrote a 2002 article titled the "Friendship Factor" in *Prevention* magazine; he revealed that "friendship has a profound effect on your physical well-being. Having good relationships improves health and lifts depressions. You don't necessarily need drugs or medical treatment to accomplish this, just friends."

This is specifically true when trying to recover from heart disease. For example, Redford B. Williams, director of the Behavioral Medicine Research Center and professor of psychiatry at Duke University Medical Center, studied 1,368 heart disease patients for more than nine years. Here are his results: "We discovered that just being married or having a good friend was a predictor of who lived and who died after a heart attack. Those patients with neither a spouse or a friend were three times more likely to die than those involved in a caring relationship."

In the medical and psychological community, the issue of having friends has become so pressing, some medical practitioners are actually suggesting likeability training. Patricia Fisher of the Rodale Center for Women's Health advised in a 2002 article, also in *Prevention,* "Make yourself likeable. Likeability is a talent . . . one we must hone."

She points to a study that links social relationships and longevity. "The first one that takes place that proves this case happened in Alameda County, California, in the late 1980s. Our researchers found over a nine-year period that the people that had the strongest social skills, community ties, and friends were the least likely to die. Not surprisingly, the others, the most isolated people, had the highest death rate of all."

One of the greatest benefits of likeability, then, is a social support system that provides you with a lifeline to help you through tough times. Consider the story of Ryan Halstead, who came into my life a few years ago when he wrote to tell me that although he had been diagnosed with cancer, he was keeping a positive attitude and trying to survive with the support of friends.

Over the course of the next year I learned a great deal about Ryan. First of all, according to his employer, Martin Doerschlag of Ohio's WD Partners, Ryan had more friends at the company than Doerschlag himself, who added, "And I own part of the place."

One day Ryan, suffering from searing pain, went to the hospital, where doctors found a tumor almost as big as a tennis ball lodged between his aorta and his lung. They gave him a low chance to live even if he opted for surgery.

"One of the reasons I was able even to have the surgery was my friends' support," Ryan says. "Many people find they're completely alone when times get bleak. I wasn't."

Besides offering support and comfort, Ryan's friends raised money to help pay for whatever bills weren't covered by his insurance. For example, WD Partners' human resources department declared that employees who put $5 in the Save Ryan Can could wear shorts instead of a suit and tie to work. And as a gesture to raise the last $5,000, Doerschlag offered to shave his long hair if the company came through with enough money. When I met Doerschlag, he was as bald as a cue ball.

Less than two months after the surgery, accompanied by forty friends, Ryan introduced himself at one of my seminars at Ohio State University. He unbuttoned his shirt to reveal a scar two feet long across his torso. Pointing to his friends, he said, "Meet my lifeline, Tim. They've made the difference between the end and the beginning."

There's truth to the old Beatles song—you'll get by with a little help from your friends. Likeable people surround themselves with a shield and a sword, a positive viewpoint of themselves and a huge collection of friends.

4

LIKEABLE PEOPLE WIN LIFE'S POPULARITY CONTESTS

We've gone over four reasons why likeability can work for every one of you. Now let's circle back to its principal benefit: *choice*.

As I mentioned, the choices *you* make don't shape your life as much as the choices *other people* make about you.

Much of your life is spent trying to get other people to pick you, whether for a job, a relationship, or a friendship, or to win a contest.

Choices occur all the time, and often they just don't seem fair. Your spouse selects a new partner. Your business partner decides to team up with someone else. Your child chooses to spend time with your ex's new spouse instead of with you. Your boss promotes a colleague with a weaker track record than yours.

Do you know why? Because all these choices belong to someone other than you, and you haven't been doing everything you can to influence them.

I've been counting the number of times that I had to make a choice concerning another person, and I've found that at least three such decisions arise each and every day.

It happens to all of us. And when we make those choices, we help determine someone else's life.

Making choices is part of being human. But although we make more and more of them, time remains constant, meaning that we have less and less of it in which to choose. Whether it's the choice to start a conversation with a stranger who could turn into a new friend or to hire a new accountant, the sheer number of choices we make conditions us to sort through all the noise and find truth as sensibly and quickly as humanly possible.

Picture the front door of a popular nightclub, where a long line of prospective partyers is waiting to go inside. The club is already full to the fire-code limit, but as a few people leave, others beg the doorman to let them enter. The more choices this doorman makes, the faster he'll make them. He'll eventually develop a set of shortcuts, a configuration of red flags, cues, and other patterns of perception connected with the club's wants and needs.

We all act like that doorman when it comes to new choices. Sometimes we lift the velvet rope, sometimes we don't. In order to understand how people make these choices, it's useful to get inside their heads to see how they deal with all the stimuli around them.

After all, if you understand and respect other people's decision-making processes, you can play to them. The good news is that most people make their choices in a predictable way.

To make choices, we go through a three-step sorting process. First, we *listen* to something out of a field of opportunities. Then we either do or do not *believe* what we've heard. Finally, we put a *value* on what we've heard.

At the end of these three steps, we make a choice.

LISTEN

The first step—and this can be quite a steep one—is to get someone to listen to our case.

By listening, I mean giving people your attention and your best effort at understanding what they have to say. You're absorbing and processing, not just hearing.

Hearing doesn't equal listening. We hear background noise all the time and pay it little heed. But when we really listen, we are working to connect with someone else.

Jon Driver, a professor at the Institute of Cognitive Neuroscience at University College in London, reviewed a century of research on the subject of attention. In a 2001 issue of the *British Journal of Psychology* he stated, "The body of research on attention suggests that our awareness of the world depends on what we choose to attend, not merely on the stimulation entering our senses."

In other words, getting in someone's face may be possible and even easy, but entering his or her attention space is what really matters.

As you've probably noticed, finding people who listen to you seems to be increasingly difficult. There's so much out there trying to find its way into our ears, and as a result we learn to ignore much of it. I believe attention may well be the newest scarce world resource.

According to Dr. Kelton Rhoads, a leading influence consultant and editor of *Working Psychology,* "We live in an environment dense with influence attempts. A large portion of the population makes a living simply getting others to comply with their requests. Conservative estimates suggest that a person will receive up to 400 persuasive appeals, just from marketers alone, in the course of a single day."

Think about it. Managers spend their time trying to influence their employees to perform. Parents spend their time trying to influence their children's behavior. Friends try to influence friends, and so on. Every one of us seems to be chattering at everyone else to get them to listen to us, to pay us attention, to think about what we have to say.

How do people deal with this information overload? They develop a filter and learn to ignore most of what they hear, and they remember even less. It's a necessary survival technique for modern life.

The late Donald Broadbent, who headed the experimental psychology unit at Cambridge University during the 1980s and early 1990s, developed a theory about this effect, based on extensive empirical research. Widely referred to as Broadbent's Filter Theory, the effect works as follows: "Humans possess a selective filter that reduces input so the brain can process other input already collected from another source. This information we put on hold, which is most of the information we perceive; and it may later be perceived to be processed, but only if it's deemed to be important. A motivation or an interest must be present later to activate that which was filtered."

We filter out the sand, and process the few pearls from everything we hear. We apply attention like a tool to understand and listen effectively. When something is important or gives us motivation, we may think about words that we initially ignored. Sometimes we're listening when we're not listening. How important we find the content to be will determine whether we give it another thought.

In the investment world, people always talk about "return on investment," or the financial profits that provide you with the incentive to put your money in a stock, bond, or other investment. Today the professional choosers of the world, be they moms or managers, brothers or brokers, demand a return on attention, too. This reality makes it increasingly difficult for people to make that first step in the choosing process: to be heard, listened to, and understood.

As a result, we have turned into a nation of professional ignorers, increasingly skilled at filtering and tuning out the noise that surrounds us—noise, unfortunately, that sometimes we should be listening to.

Director Woody Allen once remarked, "Eighty percent of life is just showing up." It's true. Being chosen in life requires showing up on other people's radar screens, getting them to hear what you say. And that happens when they choose to listen carefully.

BELIEVE

Listening is not the same thing as believing. The second step for the listener is to undergo a judgment process in which he or she determines whether or not to believe your words. This stage is the battle for acceptance.

The best way for you to achieve that acceptance is by being credible. Once people stop to listen to your case and consider the facts you present, they ask themselves: "Do I understand what's being said, and if so, does it sound credible? Does this jibe with the world as I perceive it?"

Research has found that people don't believe most of what

they hear. The late Harold Gerard, a social psychology professor at UCLA and a coauthor of the venerable college textbook *Foundations of Social Psychology,* studied the history of message acceptance, message scrutiny, and communication; he found that indeed people do not accept everything they hear as fact.

Tracing this concept of message scrutiny back to sixteenth-century French philosopher René Descartes, Gerard wrote, "In a nutshell, Descartes maintained that comprehending and the assessment of what is comprehended are distinct and separate processes. His position maintains that believing is a two-step process. Initially we comprehend some proposition about the world, and then we check it against other information and our beliefs. This is much the way a modern computer works. On the basis of comparison, we then decide to accept or reject the proposition."

You hear many statements during the course of a day, and out of the masses you hear, you probably pick only a few to believe. In 2002 Richard Edelman, CEO of Edelman Worldwide, the largest independent public-relations firm in the world, released the results from the company's fourth annual trust survey, which measured the opinions of thousands of people worldwide. According to Edelman, "Our research shows that 80 percent of those surveyed don't believe something the first time they hear, see, or read it."

Sometimes people never accept messages or claims, regardless of how many times they hear them. For example, think about your office. Do you accept everything your coworkers tell you?

The consulting firm Towers Perrin produced a 2003 study on whether employees believed what their bosses told them. The survey, which was conducted by Harris Interactive and included a cross section of workers, found that a high percentage of employees don't, in fact, believe what their boss tells them. Only 52 percent of the survey respondents believed claims about learning and development opportunities at the company; only 44 percent believed what they were told about their career opportunities; and only 39 percent believed their boss's claims about what the company would do for them if they did a good job for the company.

The pattern of disbelief holds true in our romantic lives as well. According to mid-1990s research on dating by Great Expectations, the largest and oldest dating service in the United States, "Women believe less than half of the representations they hear from their first dates, unless the date was referred to them by a trusted friend."

So if we scrutinize 50 to 80 percent of what we hear, how in the world can we decide to accept something as true?

Over time humans have learned what to believe or disbelieve through a combination of different variables. Researchers at Yale University, led by Dr. William McGuire, spent thirty years looking at these belief variables. They found that when people decide to believe a message, they first consider the source, then they consider the message; both processes are influenced by their own mood state.

For example, if your stockbroker calls you with a great investment opportunity, you will journey through this process on your way to accepting or rejecting his proposition. First you will consider the source: your stockbroker. How much credibility does he have with you? Do you trust his judgment? Second, you will think about his message. Do you understand it? Is it a believable claim? Finally, your mood will be a big determinant in your final decision. If you are in a good mood, you might be optimistic and trusting. If you are in a fearful or negative mood, you might be close-minded to any recommendations.

At times all of our claims are accepted, and at others some of our claims are disbelieved. If too much of what you say doesn't check out, you'll tip the balance and lose your credibility. As author and psychologist Charles Caldier writes in *The Persuasive Element,* "Disbelief can have a flushing effect on your argument. People may hold your proposition together, piece by piece. But if they begin to doubt the truth of what you say, they drop it immediately; or, as I like to say, flush and start over."

In the belief step, your claims move from words to facts, and a decision is ready to be made, based on the last step.

VALUE

The third step in the choice process occurs when you add up what a person has to offer. Then, based on its total value, you decide whether to choose that person and his or her proposition.

If you don't value what a person has to say, it doesn't matter if you hear and believe them. For instance, if you hear that someone wants to sell you a car, and you believe that the car is indeed an excellent value, it won't matter if you aren't in the market for a car. You don't value the information.

In the value step, you compare the potential contributions and costs of one choice against those of other choices. As you try to solve your daily problems and achieve your goals, you will usually select the people and propositions that add the most value to your life.

In its essence, your personal value to others is an equation that they can easily calculate. What is that formula? What you offer minus what you require.

Initially you present a gross value proposition, or the benefits that you offer others. People subtract from that gross value what they perceive to be your costs, or your drawbacks. What is left? Your net value, your personal bottom line in the choice process.

One of the leading voices in the field of perceived value is Dr. Jillian Sweeney, professor of marketing at the University of Western Australia. Her research has found that people assign *functional, emotional,* and *social* benefits and costs to all of the options they consider during their lives, from products to people.

Functional value is the pragmatic side of life. You are measured on your ability to perform and do something well. An employer might assume from your superior qualifications that you'll be an effective worker. A potential love interest might think you will be a good provider because you have a car, a job, and a house. Your ability to deliver the functionality others need is at the root of this type of benefit.

A functional cost, on the other hand, is your price: How much money do you require to function? How much support do you require as a friend? These are real costs that others must consider.

Emotional value is more subjective. As others consider the emotional benefits of selecting you, they move from wondering if you can perform well in your new position (functional) to wondering how you will make others feel. Bill, a doctor, recalls a situation in which he was trying to recruit a physical therapist named Michael for his facility. He was trying to convince Michael to accept his job offer, despite Michael's having received other, more lucrative offers.

During the course of the interview process, however, Bill was able to make Michael feel highly qualified and wanted. When Michael considered all of his employment options, he assigned an emotional value to Bill's offer. At that time in Michael's life, feeling wanted and admired was of primary importance.

Emotional costs represent negative feelings. If you are overly critical, have a pessimistic attitude, or scream to get what you want, you probably make others feel stupid, insecure, or anxious.

Social value concerns how you will reflect on those who choose you. As they contemplate their selection, they consider how their choice will make others feel. If you make these people look good, they are happy to receive benefits, including status, respect, and admiration.

Social costs have to do with negative reactions you bring to those who choose you. If you generate complaints, dissension, or failure, you may become a liability to your champion rather than an asset.

Let's look at some of these criteria in action. You offer your carpentry services to a neighbor whose only concern is how much you charge (functional). You interview with a harried hiring manager whose only concern is that you are low maintenance (emotional). You try out for a part in a play, and the casting director's primary goal is to select someone the other actors like (social).

This final step in the choice process can be a tough one. You must make sure you present a functional value proposition and that you are priced right for your market (personal or professional). You should be aware of your emotional appeal, which may require some observation on the part of your chooser. You too may have to consider how other people react to you and be aware of their feelings.

At the conclusion of the choice process, people will place a value on you. Then they'll do the math and compare your value to someone else's. In other words, you will be added, then subtracted, then weighed.

If you manage to create a strong set of appropriate benefits while maintaining a low set of costs, you can emerge as the best deal and win the battle of choice.

HOW LIKEABILITY MAKES A DIFFERENCE

If you've been doing a good job, you'll know how to add functional, emotional, and social value to yourself and your message, while at the same time you'll minimize your costs: the winning formula for any competition. And as already mentioned, most of life is a popularity contest.

That is why, at each step of the process, likeability can make a powerful difference.

During the listening step, your L-factor helps you get your message across to other people. They hear you, they think it over, and they remember it later.

To confirm this, consider the world of advertising. All of us watch, read, or hear scores of ads each day. The ones we listen to are the only ones that work for the advertiser. And an ad's L-factor is one of the determining reasons as to why, and how much, we listen.

Laurent Flores, a research director at IPSOS, a leading

advertising research company, conducted a 1999 North American study with an in-home system that measures consumer recall. She reported, "For all regions, the results show a positive correlation between likeability, recall and attention. The data show that likeable ads tend to better attract consumer attention, which in turn contributes to higher levels of Related Recall overall."

The strong relationship of listening to likeability is a concept supported throughout the industry. In 1994 advertising researchers David Walker and T. M. Dubitsky wrote an article in the *Journal of Advertising Research* entitled "Why Liking Matters" based on years of research. They concluded, "One of the main reasons of employing the likeability of an advertisement into the study of advertising resides in the fact that, if the consumer likes the ad he or she sees, he or she will be more likely to pay attention to it and remember the message later."

Of course, this phenomenon applies not only to the Energizer Bunny and the Budweiser Frog but to you, too. In 1997 persuasion researchers in the University of Texas's communications department conducted a study in which ten students spent an afternoon listening to twelve professors make a presentation about various subjects, none of which were part of their major.

The next day each student filled out a questionnaire, in which they rated each teacher for likeability, credibility, and authority. They also answered various true/false and multiple-choice questions about the dozen presentation topics.

The teachers rated highest on the likeability attribute also had the highest ratings for recall of the presentation's points and comprehension of its meaning. Furthermore, the teachers with the high credibility or authority marks did not win the war for attention. They took a backseat to the high L-factor teachers.

Why so? Feelings. If you make people feel great, they will listen to you, think about what you said, and store it someplace in their head.

At Pennsylvania State University, professor of psychology Karen Gasper looked at how positive and negative feelings—the fruits of likeable or unlikeable behavior—can make a difference in what we detect, decode, and store. Her body of research also suggests that generating positive feelings results in better listening and comprehension in others.

"People are aware that their intense feelings influence how they function in the world," she says. "However, they are often surprised to learn that they are influenced regularly by their everyday moods. . . . Compared to individuals in mildly sad moods, those in mildly happy moods make more positive judgments . . . , write more answers on a word association task . . . , are better at finding hidden pictures . . . , [and] are more likely to use a schema model or strategy [to] process information."

Think about it. When you're in a great mood, you're able to give more energy to understanding what's going on around you; you're more attuned, you're more interested. When you're blue, you tend to escape into the recesses of your mind; your attention span is low and your interest is lower. You are dialed out.

Our minds can deal with, and hold, only so much. But when an emotional variable such as likeability is at play, we work harder, we listen harder, and we understand even more. Yes, you might listen to negative people because their anger captures your attention and scares you. But you do it out of necessity, and you try to forget the experience as soon as possible. On the other hand, if you like someone, you give him a little space in your brain for a long time. And that is the secret of doing well in this first step of someone's choosing process: listening.

| | |

The L-factor continues to give you an edge in the next part of the choosing process: belief.

Kim Giffin, of the Communication Research Center at the University of Kansas, wrote a 1967 research review in the *Psychological Bulletin* in which he summed up years of study: "There are five characteristics of a speaker that contribute to a listener's perception of trust. They are expertness, reliability, intention, dynamicism, and likeability."

Likeability has long been viewed as a necessity in developing the trust that determines your credibility as a source. Trust and belief are created out of a desire to form a relationship and are facilitated by your likeable personality. When people are fond of you, they form a bias about you; basically, they want to believe that you are correct until proven incorrect.

Dr. Ernest Martin, a professor of advertising and personal communication at Campbell University in North Carolina, explains it this way: ". . . a commonly used source characteristic in advertising and personal selling is that of attractiveness. Attractiveness also has several sub-components including similarity, familiarity, and likability."

When people like the source of a message, they tend to trust the message or, at least, try to find a way to believe it. In other words, the positive bias created by your likeability turns a skeptic in the congregation into a member of the choir.

Another belief variable in which likeability plays an important role is the message itself. Some people may think you're credible, but your message may be hard to believe. This is where you need the benefit of the doubt, so that the chooser works hard to suspend disbelief and be willing to accept your claim.

Psychologists H. W. Berkowitz and R. J. Moyer studied argumentation, the presentation of conflicting cases, and analyzed the effect of likeability on audiences' perception of true and false. Their findings, released in the *Psychological Bulletin,* state that "when the audience likes the arguer, there's a tendency to believe the arguments that the arguer puts forward."

People won't believe anything you say just because they like you, but they will have a tendency to believe you. That can give you a huge edge.

In the early 1980s my college political science department conducted a poll to find associations between voter feelings and perceived honesty with respect to politicians' messages. We included in our survey local businesspeople, housewives, students, and teachers. We discussed politicians from other parts of the country, about whom respondents wouldn't have a preexisting attitude. We left out party affiliation and highly charged issues like religion from the information we provided about the candidates.

In the poll, voters who felt a "personal liking" or what we called "the barbecue effect" for a candidate (meaning they'd invite this person to a barbecue in their backyard) also tended to view that politician as more honest and his or her message as less deceitful than that of less likeable counterparts. Not surprisingly, the unlikeable politicians also topped the list of perceived liars.

Audiences also have a "mood state" that plays a significant role in their decision-making process. When people feel poorly, they're more skeptical. When they're satisfied, however, they're more willing to believe. This plays to likeability's strengths because likeable behavior, such as the act of saying something compassionate, delivers a good mood that sets the stage for belief. Whose mood doesn't improve when a likeable friend gives them support they feel they've otherwise been lacking?

In the world of advertising, researchers have spent years poring over data to see if likeable advertising establishes a state of belief for the messages they're trying to convey. In the late 1990s Patricia Cafferata and Alice Tybout, marketing professors at the Kellogg School of Management at Northwestern University, conducted empirical research to determine the effect of good moods on belief. They reported their findings in *Cognitive and Affective Responses to Advertising*. Among their discoveries: "Audience affect is a large area of market research in our work as it relates to belief. Information delivered with a positive emotion increases believability. . . . Our researchers have conducted warmth response studies to learn how emotional appeals are working. They have learned conclusively that claims made in the smile voice are highly effective and believed."

Ultimately, people believe what they want to believe. And they tend to believe you more if they like you.

| | |

The L-factor also gives you a leg up in the final part of the choosing process: value.

To be valued, you must offer something the other person needs.

Determining these needs can be problematic. Frequently you have to guess which of your benefits you should stress. Sometimes you find out, too late, that you've pitched the wrong one.

But if you knew exactly what others need, you'd have the blueprint for creating value in their minds.

Earlier we discussed the 2003 University of Michigan study suggesting that likeable employees are better communicators because they receive more attention from their coworkers and are able to communicate points more clearly. The same study also revealed that likeable employees receive higher-quality information about what is expected of them, as well as what is important in terms of priorities. They also enjoy more honest and detailed feedback from supervisors, coworkers, and customers, because they inspire trust as well as the willingness to tell someone what he or she needs to know to succeed.

One interviewee from my survey, a sales rep named Jenny, described a meeting with a department-store fashion buyer who was reviewing different suppliers for a new line of dresses. Part of the vendor-selection process was a printed set of requirements and specifications, such as quality and price.

Jenny, who was very likeable, was explaining her company's cost and quality advantage when the buyer interrupted to say, "Do you know what we really want, Jenny? It's not in the papers we gave out, but in all honesty, we simply want a vendor who will never miss a delivery date during Christmas."

Having this piece of information gave Jenny the opportunity to build a case for her company's dependability, while her competitors demonstrated only quality and price.

If you're likeable, you'll not only receive great information on functional needs, but you'll be able to detect other people's emotional needs as well.

Research suggests that likeability improves your capacity to understand others' emotional expressions, as well as the social implications of your own behavior. A study conducted in 1990 by psychologists Susanne Denham, Michael McKinley, and E. A. Couchoud found that "people who are liked by their peers were more able to link emotional expressions and situations and make sense of it, leading us to the conclusion that well-liked people are better able to recognize and respond to their peers' emotions."

The research concluded that likeable people are more aware of their social status, as well as the social implications of what they do, which helps them "avoid faux pas that could jeopardize their popularity and group effectiveness."

Your likeability can also convince others that, if they choose you, you can perform and deliver what they most desire. Here voting behavior is a well-studied example. We tend to value politicians because we believe that they will represent us on the issues we care about. When we like a particular politician, we assume that he or she takes the same stands on the issues as we do.

Stanford University political science professors Paul Schneiderman and Phil Tetlock, who studied voters as well as their perceptions of issues and candidates, reported their findings in their 1991 book *Explorations in Political Psychology*. "Voters infer stands to individuals by attributing their own views to individuals they like," they said. "They also attribute opposing views and issues to candidates that they dislike."

For example, if you favor the space program and you like candidate Johnnie Johnson, you will assume she is also prospace program. Only a direct statement to the contrary from her will change your mind. That's why so many voters, using like-ability as a shortcut, believe that their favorites believe in their values. As I mentioned earlier, Gallup's personality factor poll, conducted prior to every presidential election since 1960, has found that only one of three factors (issues, party affiliation, and likeability) has been a consistent prognosticator of the final election result. That factor is likeability.

Likeability as a mental shortcut for perceived functional value has also been shown in the field of advertising. August Busch IV, the president of Anheuser-Busch, was once asked to discuss the major effect of Budweiser's commercials over the previous ten years. "When the viewer likes your ad or your brand," he said, "they assume you make a high-quality product."

Decades of focus group research support this claim: Like-ability is a shortcut for quality. "I like you; you can perform" is a common association for all of us, whether or not it is supported by the facts.

For those looking for emotional rather than practical benefits from you, your likeability will help convince them that you will add value to their emotional environment—almost as if you were creating it. Psychologist William Benson, who wrote a 1995 paper on the subject of emotions and environment, observed that "pleasant, highly likeable people bring joy and happiness into the lives of others in almost every context. They create a credible promise of an emotionally rewarding experience by their very nature. All of the things that they do reinforce the idea that they can be depended on by their friends and loved ones to be a pick-me-up in an otherwise negative and hostile world."

When you're likeable, the promise of good emotional times

accompanies you. Interviewee Ray, a tax attorney, was competing for a new client named Larry, who was in trouble with the IRS and feeling stressed. The other lawyers Larry had met had made him feel even more anxious and unhappy. He needed someone who could calm him as well as do his taxes competently. That person had to have a great desk-side manner—which the highly personable and empathetic Ray possessed in spades. So although Ray might not have been the very best tax attorney available, he was the only one who met Larry's emotional needs. He got the job.

Still other people are looking for fulfillment of their social needs—they need their decisions to be respected. Psychologist and author John Kinnell studied the relationship between likeability and group popularity in adults. In his 1997 paper "The Roots of Popularity," he wrote, "Likeability was the greatest predictor of popularity and social acceptance in a group for adults, more important than wealth, status, or physical attractiveness."

Likeability helps you send signals to others that you will continue to be likeable once you have been selected, producing social value by helping the selector look as though he or she made an excellent choice and will continue to make good choices in the future.

Interviewee Dave explains how he considered popularity when making a recommendation for his replacement in his local PTA. Although he didn't want to admit it, he wanted his peers on the committee to remember him not just as a good committee member but as one who found a popular successor. This was why, when Dave made his choice, he picked someone who wasn't necessarily the most qualified but who made everyone else happy.

If you are likeable, you will find you're often the best choice with the fewest costs. You haven't given anyone reason to believe that you will produce emotional or social problems in the future. You don't send out any warning signals to indicate that you'll have a negative attitude, or a temper tantrum, or repeated fights. Instead, you're perceived as creating warm feelings and positive attitudes. You're seen as conscientious, as well as emotionally and socially mature.

Your likeable personality will always improve your overall value. By reducing uncertainties, it allows your benefits to shine in the final analysis.

Here's an illustration of the three-step choice process from my own life. In 2000 my division of Yahoo! was considered among the top places in the company to work. So when I posted a want ad for an executive briefing consultant—whose job it would be to ponder the future while traveling around the globe—the applications flowed in. Soon aggressive candidates were calling me every day.

Of all the applicants, one young man named Richard captured my attention every time he called or wrote. There was something friendly and pleasant about his voice; I found myself *listening* to him immediately and easily. He pierced the armor.

I was still listening to several other applicants, too. I just wasn't sure I believed everything they said. They all talked the talk, pointing out their many accomplishments, but I couldn't help but view their claims with a jaundiced eye. With Richard, however, something told me that his accomplishments were pertinent to the job at hand. I *believed* him.

I flew him across the country to visit me at Yahoo!'s headquarters. His face just beamed as he talked about the job opportunity. When I talked about its challenges and requirements, I found his attitude open and engaging.

In our face-to-face meeting, he asked me about my upcoming travels and account assignments. I painted him a harried and horrific picture of constant travel, late nights of report-gathering, and mounting workloads. He then looked me straight in the eye and said, "Let me help you. Let me take some of this work for you. You're going to kill yourself on this schedule."

At that moment I realized that of all the candidates, I *valued* him the most. I could see that he truly was going to help me. And because I valued his potential more than anyone else's, I chose him for the job.

Most of the other candidates had legitimate credentials for the position, but Richard's high L-factor was his trump card in this fairly typical hiring scenario.

| | |

Now that you understand how the L-factor works, you'll need to know something else equally important: It's possible to improve your L-factor.

Your likeability is not static. It is an ongoing process. Everyone's L-factor moves up and down. Five today, seven tomorrow.

Many of us think that when others change their mind about our likeability, it's their problem. We're the constant—they're the ones who shift.

But if we had neon signs hanging above our heads that posted our current L-factor, we would see it move up and down like the stock market. That dim-witted joke you just told your officemates dropped you from a five to a four; that sweet favor you did for your bedridden cousin upped you from a six to a seven.

If that sign really existed, it would probably stop us from indulging in so many obnoxious habits. We wouldn't break so many rules of basic human relations. We wouldn't do half the dumb things we do. But we've never been taught how to install that imaginary sign above our head; it's a fantasy out of *Psychology Today* meets *Popular Mechanics*.

But what if we did know how? What if we became sufficiently aware not just of ourselves but of other people's feelings, so that we perceived, in real time, the fluctuation of our L-factor? It would fundamentally rewire our actions as well as the very way we think. We would be able to see the damage that we do when we are unlikeable.

We may not have that sign, but we do have the next best thing: a brain that allows us to examine patterns in our lives.

If someone suddenly tells you, "I don't want to be your friend anymore," and it's an aberration, it may indeed be that person's problem. But if you notice a pattern in which people move from liking to disliking you, and you find yourself surprised again and again by this development, you should worry about your L-factor.

What specific steps should you take? How can you raise your L-factor? Read on, and you'll find out.

Part Two

RAISING YOUR L-FACTOR

5

THE FOUR ELEMENTS
OF LIKEABILITY

Now that you have grasped what a big difference the L-factor can make in your personal and professional lives, have seen how life can be a popularity contest, and understand how people make choices, it's time to put likeability to work for you. The best way to start is by looking at its basic components.

Let's begin with a story about my son Anthony. From the time he was six years old, Anthony wanted to play the guitar. Within a couple of years he could improvise a few tunes; when he turned thirteen, I gave him a subscription to *Guitar Heroes* magazine. The next year I bought him an amplifier.

Despite all his interest and equipment, Anthony wasn't very good. He didn't make music as much as he made noise—lots and lots of noise. He seemed lost. I was lost, too.

Finally, four months ago, I did what I should have done in the first place. I signed him up for lessons at the local guitar store.

Anthony's teacher, Tad, immediately steered him to the most important fundamental: He deconstructed the instrument.

First, Tad taught Anthony how to tune the guitar so he could better understand its sounds. Then he taught him how to play chords, so that Anthony could easily assemble songs based on simple constructions. Finally, he taught him how to play scales, so he could hear the guitar's full range.

In the past few months Anthony's playing has improved more than during the previous five years. Because he now understands the instrument's fundamentals, he can master its music.

When we grasp something's basic mechanics, we gain insight into how it works, and why. This understanding is as necessary for music as it is for golf, salesmanship, painting—and likeability.

One of the reasons likeability is so often crudely implemented is that nearly all of us need lessons in its inner workings, just as we would if we wanted to learn how to play the guitar. No one has ever explained how to tune our personality, or taught us the chords we can strike to resonate with other people. We don't understand how to create the melodies that will entice other people to care for us.

But if you take the time to understand and learn likeability's basics, you'll be able to move on to the specifics of raising your L-factor.

Bear with me now as we shift metaphors and gears, from the guitar to the car.

Let's say you're driving along an isolated road, and you hit a stoplight. This first light represents *friendliness*.

If you are not friendly, the light remains red and you can't go any further. If you are friendly, the light turns green and you drive on.

Friendliness is the most fundamental element of likeability; if you are not friendly, you will have to work exponentially harder to be likeable. Some people are able to do this—we all have had at least one irascible friend whom we nonetheless love. But we don't have many; there isn't enough time.

Back inside the car, imagine that you're driving along the highway again and arrive at a second stoplight. This one stands for *relevance*.

If you can find a way to be relevant to someone else, you get a green light and can drive on. Otherwise, the light stays red. That smiling, sweet doorman may be the friendliest man you've ever met, but if your building is across the street from his, and you have no contact with him, you don't really care whether he's friendly.

Now, in the car again, you hit a third light; this one represents *empathy*. If you are able to prove that you are an empathetic person who understands, and in a way actually senses, another person's feelings, you get a green light and can keep on driving. Empathy is possibly the least understood of the four factors, yet without it your friendliness and relevance will have a hard time finding a sustainable place in another person's heart.

There's one more stoplight, and this one stands for *realness*. Some people, in trying to boost their L-factor, seem genuinely friendly, relevant, and empathetic. But eventually you discover there's no one there; it's all an act. Over time you wonder, "Is this person for real?" If he or she isn't, then you have reached the end of the line.

Of course, most of us aren't conscious of these four lights. When we meet someone new, we seldom actually ask ourselves, "Is this person relevant, and if so, is he or she empathetic?"

While we're engrossed in the middle of life, we're not thinking about every little detail we've learned. We simply combine

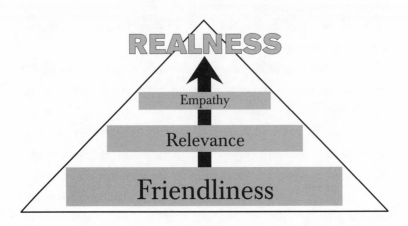

all our information and talents and act, as when we drive a car or perform other skills we've mastered.

Similarly, when we meet a new person, we don't pause to deliberate about each element of his or her likeability factor. Yet for the most part, we won't become likeable to someone else, nor will that person be likeable to us, unless all four criteria are met.

You can probably credit this pattern to the human survival instinct. Since our cave days, we've needed to be able to tell the difference between the likeable and the unlikeable, friend or foe. Knowing whom to like made our existence easier. Many aeons later, it still does. This ability is, as my anthropology teacher used to say, baked into our bones.

Now it's time to go over each one of these four aspects in depth.

FRIENDLINESS

A reporter once asked physicist Albert Einstein what question he would ask the universe if he were guaranteed an honest and direct reply. Einstein's answer came swiftly, as though he had been pondering the question for a long time: "Is the universe friendly?"

The rest of us think about friendliness, too. But rather than asking whether the larger universe is friendly, we ask whether the universe immediately surrounding us is. Will other people be friendly to us?

Friendliness is the first element we consider when we meet someone new. It's the threshold of likeability.

By *friendly,* I mean "expressing a liking for another person," or "communicating welcome," or "expressing a generally positive feeling." Friendly messages can convey "I enjoy your company," "I am happy to see you," or simply "I'm open to your being here."

On the other hand, unfriendliness is the communication of negative feelings through verbal and/or nonverbal methods. Unfriendly messages convey "You aren't welcome," "You irritate me," or "I'm closed to your presence."

It is human nature to seek friendliness as a prerequisite for liking someone. Communication expert Bert Decker, who works with thousands of businesspeople, salespeople, and educators, says, "If you want to get your message across, you must reach and connect with the first brain. You must first persuade the listener's first brain that you represent warmth, comfort, and safety. . . . Whenever we communicate, our listener's Gatekeeper [the first brain] is right there on guard, figuratively asking, 'friend or foe?'"

The "first brain" is the equivalent of a receptionist who prevents others from getting their feet in the door to sell themselves to you.

Here's an example of the Gatekeeper at work. A few years

ago at a crowded cocktail party, I spotted a local artist whose work I admire. When I finally met him, I told him so openly, with respect. Up until that point the man had seemed thoroughly bored by the party. But now he stopped, turned, and engaged me in a serious talk about art for fifteen minutes. It's as if that receptionist inside his head had said, "Mister Sanders is here to see you now."

The Gatekeeper can also work against you. An unfriendly first encounter can create a long, long road to establishing likeability. One interviewee from my survey, Billy, talked about a problem he had with one of his college professors. He met the professor while he was working at a part-time summer job in an electronics store. A man brought in a high-tech clock radio/CD player that he wasn't able to operate. Billy, thinking it was the world's most user-friendly device, was unfriendly throughout the exchange, making it clear he felt the man was a techno-idiot.

Eight weeks later, walking into his first anthropology class, Billy realized his professor was the man with the clock radio. Unfortunately, the man remembered Billy as well. If looks could kill, Billy would have been dead on the spot. Billy tried to make it clear to the professor that he was a good student and a good kid. But the man shut down. The real lesson Billy learned from that particular class was that random acts of unfriendliness can come back to bite you in the rear.

After all, our first instinct when someone is friendly is to reciprocate. If you perceive that someone likes you, you're more willing to like them back. A friendship becomes possible.

Remember when you were young and the doctor would tap your knee with a little rubber hammer, causing it to jerk forward?

That's called a reflex reaction. We have social reflexes as well. When someone taps you with a friendliness hammer, you react.

A vast number of studies have been published on this subject. For example, Dr. Theodore Newcomb, chairman of the doctoral program in social psychology at the University of Michigan, studied the like/dislike phenomenon in human nature for more than ten years. In his landmark book *Group Dynamics Research and Theory,* he cited reciprocation as one of the main reasons that people like or dislike each other.

The work of Charles Faulkner, author of *The Technology of Achievement,* also confirms our innate tendency to reciprocate. "Social influence works because we're social creatures," Faulkner says. "We respond to authority, notice friendliness, try to reciprocate, keep our commitments."

Have you ever wondered why a waiter sometimes leaves small pieces of candy with the check? It's designed to elicit reciprocation. A team of university researchers led by Bruce Rind at Temple University concluded that diners who are provided these small gifts of candy tended to perceive the server as friendly and reciprocate with a larger tip.

In another example, Charles Pavitt, professor of interpersonal/organizational communication at the University of Delaware, led an experiment in one of his psychology classes. He found that "one of the most important factors in the degree to which Cisco, a subject here, for example, likes Kristen, another student, is the degree to which Kristen likes Cisco. . . . There are many possible reasons that Cisco will tend to reciprocate Kristen's liking. The approval that Cisco gets from Kristen as a sole factor could cause Cisco to return Kristen's liking. And, in addition, Cisco can look forward to cooperation and support from Kristen. This adds even more to Cisco's reciprocation."

Conversely, unfriendliness lowers likeability. An act of rudeness or angry outbursts can send an L-factor of seven plummeting to a four. Author and researcher Dr. William Cottringer conducted a three-year survey of several thousand people in St. Louis that focused on why people like or dislike others. The study revealed that the ultimate act of unfriendliness is a display of anger.

I've learned firsthand how an angry outburst, aka a temper tantrum, can pin the unfriendly label on you and kill your L-factor. When I was in the second grade, my best friend was a boy named Curtis who lived on the farm adjacent to ours. Every weekend we'd play football, tag, cards, or whatever game we could invent.

One Saturday morning I wanted to see a movie downtown, but my mom had a rule: Someone's got to go with you. Curt, the only guy around, preferred to stay home and play cards. So that's what we did, but I fumed the entire time. Finally we had a misunderstanding about the score, and I blew up, waving my arms hysterically and overturning the table. Curt walked home as fast as he could. Realizing that I'd upset him, I ran after him, apologizing. But he waved me off with one hand.

Meanwhile my mom, who had been watching all of this from the front porch, warned me, "Every time you get ugly with someone, somebody's going to get hurt. Usually it's going to be you. A fit like this wipes out all the great things you've done over the last few years. For some time now Curtis is going to see you through ugly eyes."

Unfriendly acts don't just make you see others through ugly eyes; they create havoc within your body, too. Unfriendliness manufactures what researchers call a "negative emotional experience."

Here's how it works. When someone behaves in an unfriendly manner toward you, your brain sends a signal to your body's command centers to react by deploying hormones. As bestselling author Deepak Chopra says, "Where a thought goes, a chemical follows."

Two hormones are especially relevant to your emotional state: DHEA (dehydroepiandrosterone) and cortisol. Think of DHEA as the feel-good hormone, while cortisol makes you feel stressed out.

When you encounter unfriendliness, your cortisol level increases, prompting the symptoms of stress. You can feel a rush of blood to your face, a sudden heat, a pounding chest, the sweats, and perhaps even minor shaking.

This spike in your cortisol level doesn't make you feel bad only when the problem occurs. Over time, as you encounter the unfriendly person over and over, it can lead to chronic problems, from a poor immune system to increased blood pressure.

On the other hand, friendliness creates a positive emotional experience, as well as a positive physical reaction. Your DHEA increases, decreasing your stress and slowing down your heart rate. This is why simple acts of friendliness can make you feel as if you have the wind beneath your wings.

One of the survey interviewees, Miranda, remembers taking piano lessons as a child from a hostile teacher who made her feel unwelcome in her house—so unwelcome that Miranda would go home feeling sick after every lesson. Eventually she even felt ill before each lesson, so much so that she begged her parents to let her stop. Miranda eventually switched instruments and today is a violinist with her city's symphony orchestra. One reason she did well with the violin, she says, was her next teacher's friendliness. He made her feel so welcome that she felt good being around him and practiced extra hard to please him.

When people are friendly and positive to us, we feel great and enjoy their presence. The validity of this theory was demonstrated in a 2000 study of more than twenty-five hundred high school students, conducted by Stanford researcher and management consultant Van Sloan.

Sloan, in collaboration with many school systems across the country, conducted several years' worth of surveys that attempted to gauge the relationship between popularity and personality traits. The traditional thinking was that the dominant factors in popularity were attractiveness, intelligence, and/or athletic ability.

Sloan's results showed something else: "Students have a better chance of becoming more likeable by practicing the traits that correlational analysis in this study show are important social skills. These traits include general happiness; an upbeat, positive personality; smiling; and really liking most people. Surprisingly, physical attractiveness and going along with the crowd were negative factors or insignificant in the student's social popularity in the classrooms we measured. For example, for females, number of smiles per day was two times more significant to their popularity than physical attractiveness. All in all . . . friendliness is foundational to getting along with other people and being preferred throughout your life."

The late actor John Ritter, star of the 1970s situation comedy *Three's Company,* is an excellent example of how friendliness fosters likeability. Ritter, son of country musician Tex Ritter, was interviewed a few years ago for the alumni publication of the University of Southern California. When the reporter asked, "Why are you so easygoing and friendly? Isn't L.A. a dog-eat-dog town?" Ritter replied, "I realized that if I was easygoing and good-natured, I'd still get most of the parts I deserved and be happy in the end. I wanted to act, and I wanted to live a life with a family, not fight with the world."

Friendliness wasn't just something Ritter talked about—everyone witnessed it. After his death in 2003, fans and fellow actors wrote thousands of testimonials on the Web and in magazines. Actor Gino Marrocco said, "John Ritter is exactly the same as he was on the show [*Three's Company*] . . . very friendly, very warm." Television producer Thomas Watson observed, "He was as friendly to us little folk in production as he was to the fellow performers and stars."

Friendliness was the cornerstone of Ritter's success. It became part of his on-screen persona, and the public responded to it. According to television historian R. D. Heldenfels, "Most of his success came from that friendliness. Ritter didn't just play likeable. He often was, off-camera, when he did not have to be, the nicest person I ever worked with. There is no mystery to John Ritter's appeal. People just liked him."

When you are friendly, others want to be with you, and they want you to succeed. Your message, "I like you; I'm open to you," is reciprocated by their message, "I like you, too." Without this initial friendliness, likeability is not likely to happen.

RELEVANCE

Driving down the likeability highway, you come to the next stoplight. With friendliness you asked, "Friend or foe?" Here you ask, "So what?"

You need to know how important the other person will be in your life. Your mind is making the transition from seeking safety to seeking significance.

Even when people are very friendly, you have little reason to care about them if they have little bearing on your life. Someone must also be relevant to your life if your relationship is to pass through the next stoplight.

Relevance is the extent to which the other person connects to your life's interests, wants, and needs. Sergio Zyman, the former chief marketing officer at Coca-Cola, spent his career thinking about what keeps a person, a brand, or even a company relevant over time. When you are relevant, he maintains, you've connected to someone's sweet spot—that area of our hearts and minds in which our passions are concentrated, the bull's-eye in each of us that represents something very significant.

Every one of us has at least one, if not many, sweet spots. One of my own personal sweet spots is stress relief. I spend so much of my time running from one part of the world to another that whenever people can help me relax, they hit my sweet spot dead on. Anyone who shows up in my life and makes it less stressful will be potentially relevant to me.

Here's an example. Let's say you've been particularly worried about your personal finances. You go to a party and meet an accountant who clearly can help you manage your money in a way you never dreamed possible. That person has shot an arrow right into the bull's-eye of your sweet spot.

Of course, some people will always be more relevant to you than others. The variable is the strength of the connection. When people connect with one of your high-level interests or needs, their relevance to you soars.

Conversely, when people connect with a trivial interest or need, they are less relevant.

Several years ago at an Internet conference, before I went to Yahoo!, I met the president of Yahoo! Brazil, Bruno Fiorentini. We got along well, but as time passed we didn't make much effort to sustain the relationship—neither of us had the time or the motivation.

I saw Bruno again when I went to work for Yahoo!, and whenever he was on campus we'd wave at each other. He still wasn't particularly relevant to my life—until my boss asked me to give a speech in São Paolo, Brazil. Then Bruno's relevance jumped exponentially. I no longer simply chatted with him; now he established my agenda—where I'd stay, where I'd eat—and even arranged my security. Today I talk to him often. He's my Brazilian connection, a huge solution in my life.

For the most part, relevance has three levels, or degrees: contact, mutual interests, and value. Each delivers distinct psychological benefits that boost likeability.

On the most basic level, someone becomes relevant to you simply by walking onto your life's path. The University of Michigan's Theodore Newcomb defines this event as "basic contact."

In 1961 Newcomb conducted an experiment on a form of contact that he labeled the "acquaintance process." He arranged to use a boardinghouse near the university's Ann Arbor campus and invited seventeen male transfer students to live there for a semester, free of charge. In exchange, the students were required to participate in several hours' worth of research each week. During this time Newcomb performed various experiments examining the patterns of friendship that soon formed among the young men.

Newcomb discovered that "functional distance was one of the major determinants in liking." Students were attracted to students who sat with them in class and seemed to like them.

As Newcomb points out, many studies prior to this experiment showed that friendships at school or work are more likely to form when people sit near each other, as opposed to far away from each other, in the same room. This is also true of people who live near each other.

A study inspired by Newcomb's experiment and conducted by Princeton psychology professor John Darley also illustrates the positive effects of closeness.

A group of women were brought together purportedly to discuss their dietary habits. The researchers gave them information about a fictional female who was to become their experiment partner, and also about another fictional woman who would be joining the general discussion. The researchers then asked the women to evaluate both new participants. The women expressed more liking for their new partner than for the new discussion participant, despite the fact that the information they received about the two was identical.

| | |

A higher level of relevance is established through *mutual interests*. People become relevant to you when you share a hobby (whether it's an appreciation of jazz, backpacking, or poetry), a friend or relative, or a political or religious belief.

People with whom you enjoy a mutual interest can make you feel validated, as well as provide a sense of community. If you and I are both enthused about stamp collecting, I will be relevant to you. You realize that you're not the only crazy person in the world who spends hours poring over little colored pieces of paper. You now have someone to talk to, someone to share your feelings.

Alan Hudin and his staff at the Relationship Dynamics Institute, working with researchers from the University of Vermont, tested the connection between mutual interests and liking. Prior to the study, the researchers asked participants to provide personal information about their interests, goals, and hobby activities.

During the experiment the participants were given a series of informational points on six fictional people, whom they were asked to rate. Three of the fictional people had at least one point of common interest with each participant, and three did not. Other than their shared interests, the attributes of all six were very similar.

The participants rated those with a common interest significantly higher than those without. When a fictional person shared two or more interests, both the liking and approval ratings were even higher.

Such outcomes are quite typical. Lani Arredondo, a corporate consultant to hundreds of Fortune 500 firms, has spent decades monitoring mutual interest and its effect on our emotions. "It's a characteristic of human nature," she says. "We prefer dealing with people who are like us. It's easier to understand one another when we share some things in common, a common language, similar backgrounds, common interests. Commonality unites people and reduces conflict."

|||

Relevance is strongest when a personal *value* proposition that you offer connects with another person's wants and needs. If you possess a skill that will help someone complete a task, you are relevant to that person. If you appeal to someone's need to laugh, your relevance is your sense of humor. Your value produces positive attitudes in other people's minds about you and raises your L-factor.

In 2001 researchers at the Management Performance Institute, working in conjunction with the University of Arizona, conducted an experiment to test this question: Does power make you well liked? Sixteen workers from an aerospace manufacturing company were introduced to three subjects via videotape. Before watching the videotape, they were given a short description of the name, title, and function of each of the three subjects at the company.

According to the description, the first subject was soon to become the next quality-review officer, who would examine each worker's performance at year's end. This review would impact each study participant's compensation, bonus, and promotion potential.

The second subject was a quality-review officer for another division of the company, unrelated to the workers' appraisals.

The third subject was an entry-level worker in a different division of the company.

All three subjects had similar mannerisms and attitudes and made similar statements. Each worker rated the three subjects for likeability, sincerity, and intelligence. In all but one case, the workers rated the first subject (their future quality-review officer) as most likeable. And in all cases, the subjects rated this man the person with whom they'd most like to have lunch.

| | |

When you connect with people's wants and needs, your L-factor increases. As the Arizona experiment demonstrates, as your importance grows, so does your likeability. It's as though your personal stock price rose in their soul's marketplace. People are utilitarian. They relate to things that are important. And when you find a way to matter, you're locked and loaded, suited and booted, and ready to go.

On the other hand, irrelevance can create ambivalence—you don't tend to feel much for a person who's not relevant to you. University of Auckland psychologist Fram Dalstead says, "People measure their emotions along the lines of personal pertinence. . . . Most people hold back strong feelings until you are significant, and then there is an experience of flooding, meaning you have tremendous feelings, the more important someone is to your life."

In telling the story of his failed marriage, interviewee Greg described how his irrelevance killed his L-factor with his wife. "When we were first married, we had a great deal in common," Greg says. "We were each other's best friend. All that began to change after five years—our interests shifted; we grew apart. I became fascinated with computers and no longer spent my spare time with my wife looking at antiques, which we did for the first few years of our marriage. Meanwhile, she became interested in spirituality. We had disagreements and even arguments about the importance of each other's passions. She said I made her feel bad about herself. I felt she found me trivial and shallow. We completely lost our connection."

Another interviewee, Carolyn, described a situation concerning her best friend from high school. "I always loved Elaine. She was the gossip grapevine queen. Our school motto was 'telephone, telefax, tell Elaine.' She knew who was dating who, who was fighting with who, all the essential stuff."

Carolyn went away to college, married, and started a family, while Elaine remained in their hometown, single. When Carolyn recently moved back with her two children, she and Elaine tried to reignite their friendship. "Elaine is still the queen of gossip, she's still involved with the dating scene. It's all she wants to talk about." Carolyn doesn't relate anymore. In her world, Elaine moved from being necessary to being noisy, and Carolyn began to see her less and less. When she noticed Elaine's phone calls on caller ID, she let them go to voice mail. Carolyn concluded, "I'm only passionate about people who are pertinent."

Ultimately, relevance is a connection that serves as an important L-factor building block. Relevance is like wind to a sailboat. When it's missing, the potential for high L-factor disappears, too.

Consider the characters in J. R. R. Tolkien's *The Lord of the Rings*. Along with one human, Aragorn, come Frodo (a Hobbit), Gandalf (a powerful wizard), Gimli (an ax-wielding dwarf), and Legolas (an arrow-shooting elf). None of these characters would have been likeable to one another if they hadn't been bound by a common interest. Realizing that their mission will make all the difference to Middle Earth, these disparate characters form the Brotherhood of the Ring to fight the terrible evil represented by the villain, Sauron.

Because of the ring and their common mission to fight for good, the members of this strange group of creatures are highly relevant to one another. This relevance creates friendships that would otherwise never have occurred. Frodo and his fellow Hobbits would have had no reason to make friends with creatures who lived outside their homeland. Gimli's and Legolas's people are sworn enemies, and in fact the two start off disliking each other. But the need to band together overcomes their initial antagonism, and the two eventually become more like brothers than enemies. Likewise, the elderly Gandalf probably would have no reason to be friends with any of the others if not for the ring.

It's not likely that any of us will one day find a ring that will lead us to a life-or-death battle to save the entire world from evil. But we may well find someone with a relevant interest that helps us form a bond with him or her. When that happens, we're well on the way to likeability.

EMPATHY

Okay, you've sped past the lights that stand for friendliness and relevance. Now you're at the empathy stoplight.

Once you've decided that another person is friendly and relevant, you begin to wonder, consciously or unconsciously, if that person understands you. Can he see things from your point of view? Can she feel what you feel?

When I was growing up, I worked as a cook at a hot-dog stand called (believe it or not) Der Wienerschnitzel. The owner had a strict policy that if an employee made a mistake, whether it was blowing an order, botching paperwork, or just reporting late for work, they had to wear a paper hat with the word STUPID spelled out in big red letters on its rim.

Whenever I wore the hat (which happened much more often than I wanted), customers made fun of me, and I'd feel terrible. But no matter how many times we employees protested, the owner wouldn't reverse his policy. "Stupid people deserve to be known as stupid," he'd mutter.

One day the owner sold the place and a new boss, Jed, appeared on the scene. Guess what I wanted Jed to know right away?

Jed turned out to be highly empathetic. He not only listened to our complaints about the hat, he spent an entire shift working next to me and the other employees. He even wore the STUPID hat so he could get a sense of what life was like for those forced to sport it.

Needless to say, he soon eliminated the stupid rule.

What Jed was able to do was empathize with my situation. What does that signify? According to renowned psychologist Carl Rogers, empathy is the ability to perceive another person's internal frame of reference with accuracy.

As defined by the *American Heritage Dictionary,* empathy represents an "identification with and understanding of another's situation, feelings, and motives."

To these descriptions I would add that empathy is the ability to imagine yourself in the place of another and, from that vantage point, to be able to understand his or her feelings, desires, ideas, and/or actions, good or bad.

It's not only about comprehending others' factual circumstances, but also, in some form, about actually experiencing their feelings.

Empathy is different from sympathy. If you are sympathetic to others, your heart goes out to them and you feel compassion, but these are *your* feelings. You don't know what *they're* feeling. You're not trying to know. You're simply feeling bad that others feel bad (or lonely, or depressed, or angry).

If you are empathetic to others, however, you are not merely feeling sorry for them but are projecting yourself into their hearts, as though you are sensing what it's like to be in their shoes.

Sympathy is a sweet emotion, but it's not a connecting one. It doesn't give you the awareness of the other person that creates a bond, the identification that helps create true likeability.

What does it feel like to be on the receiving end of empathy? It's not as if you can read someone else's mind and know that he or she feels your pain. But you can sense when others really do understand what's going on inside your head by their reactions. My old boss, Jed, proved it by seeing how bad I felt at work and fixing it.

Here's another example. Have you ever been in a situation in which someone keeps referring to you in a way you resent? Let's say your mom introduces you to all her friends as her "little baby," even though you're twenty-five years old and living on your own. You hate it, but she does it over and over.

Finally you protest, explaining that her words make you feel childish. Although she seems confused at first ("But you *are* my little baby . . ."), you finally get her to understand your feelings. Lo and behold, something magical happens. Your mom introduces you to her friends by your name. Even though she doesn't want to make the change, she empathizes with your embarrassment, and once that happens, she wouldn't dream of making you feel bad.

Where empathy is absent, the opposite occurs. Have you ever broken up with a lover and then told one of your friends about it, only to have him or her blurt out, "It's just as well–I never liked him much anyway"?

By just self-referentially telling you about his or her own emotions, that person is not being sensitive to your feelings of loss, much less to your original feelings of attachment. After such an encounter, you end up with a sense of emptiness. That's what a lack of empathy feels like.

On the other hand, a sensitive friend, finding out about your failed relationship, might look into your heart and ask, "Doesn't that make you feel like you've lost something?" or "You really feel alone now, don't you?" This conversation can produce a positive feeling inside you, knowing that somebody else understands your emotional state.

Empathy enhances likeability because it delivers many such psychological benefits, including a sense of personal worth, clarity, and relief. When someone takes the time to find out, and talk through, exactly how you feel, your self-esteem rises. You feel not only appreciated but validated and less alone. There's a sense of connection. It's as though this person were a student of you.

Whenever I meet highly empathetic people, I enjoy experiencing their skills in the same way I delight in hearing a good singer's beautiful voice. Such people will say something that indicates that they know exactly what I'm feeling and that they feel it too, and I feel better as a result.

Sympathy can be faked. "I feel so bad for you" is easy to say because there's no way to check its accuracy. But empathy is almost impossible to fake, because you can't fake true understanding of another's feelings. Nor can you fake the feeling it creates. You can tell the difference between someone who pretends to know how you feel and someone who says something so insightful that he or she seems to have been inside your head and, instead of guessing, appears to be reporting on what he or she sees.

Carl Rogers's groundbreaking *Client-Centered Therapy* states that when a client receives empathetic understanding from his physician or psychologist, he or she is able to trust and understand himself or herself better and can more easily make beneficial behavioral changes.

Rogers writes, "When conditions of deep, empathetic care are authentically embraced and applied by health practitioners, a climate of change and self-actualization will be created in the patients."

Since this book was published in the 1950s, more than four hundred university and clinical studies have confirmed its thesis.

The positive environment engendered by empathy isn't found only in the doctor's office—it's everywhere. According to psychologist Lawrence Bookbinder, a fellow in the division of psychotherapy of the American Psychological Association, "A conversation partner who's being empathically acknowledged sometimes feels like she or he is being hugged."

Bookbinder uses an example from his own private practice. Two women, Tanya and Anita, engage in an empathetic conversation. Tanya is having a difficult time admitting to Anita (and herself) that she's fallen in love with her boyfriend. She's never been in love before, and the idea causes mixed emotions. Anita senses something is wrong and encourages Tanya to talk about it. For the first time, Tanya is able to articulate her feelings under the guidance of her empathetic friend, who feels the confusion in Tanya's heart and helps her sort through the anxiety it has created.

"Tanya experiences Anita's use of empathy," says Dr. Bookbinder. "These are gifts . . . of time, attention, not being interrupted, not being criticized. And the experience Tanya has in receiving these gifts is the same as receiving affection." As a result, they become tightly bonded.

Empathetic friends make you feel special. They help you sense your own value, that you're worth taking the time to understand.

Empathy provides another likeability advantage. Many people have difficulty expressing their feelings. If you're one of them, empathy can help others find a voice for your emotions. When someone not only takes the time to find out how you feel but also helps you put those feelings into words, you receive a sense of clarity. Your feelings are no longer rumbling about inarticulately in your head; you now can hear them, think about them, and work with them.

In the movie *Good Will Hunting,* young Will enters therapy because of a troubled history of abuse. In his sessions with his therapist, Dr. Maguire, a series of empathetic conversations ensue after the doctor shares a dark secret—he too had been abused as a child.

Because he truly understands Will's feelings, Dr. Maguire can figuratively jump into Will's mind and enunciate to Will his own feelings, which Will soon utters aloud for the first time. Through these conversations, Will focuses on a single word that describes how he really feels: *innocent*. He was never at fault; he was a good kid—good Will Hunting. This powerful realization unleashes Will's potential, giving him the freedom to live life as he wishes.

When I think about the most likeable and unlikeable characters in my own life, I remember Timmy, a friend's older brother. A fine musician, Timmy moved to Los Angeles and become an instant success—he always got gigs and made a good deal of money.

One day Timmy was visiting his brother in Tucson, where I was living, and I talked to him about my career frustration. My band had played only fifteen shows in the previous year, and even those had been sparsely attended. Regardless of how much we practiced and promoted our shows, we couldn't generate a dedicated following.

When I told this to Timmy, he simply shrugged his shoulders and said, "Let me tell you about my experience. If you rock, the crowds will double every week and someone will offer you a deal. No way I'd do fifteen gigs without having a big crowd. You're in a real bad place there."

To this day I still remember how terrible I felt after that conversation.

In contrast, a week later I met a musician named Joe, the bass player in a successful local reggae band. I shared my problems with Joe, too. Although he was also successful, Joe, trying hard to understand how I felt, blurted out how uncomfortable he knew it must be to stand in front of those small crowds and how bad he felt for me. Was there anything he could do to help?

For years I basked in the glow of his kindness, and his likeable personality helped me accept some of his advice, no matter how difficult. Frankly, he suggested I take voice lessons. I swallowed my pride and did it. My performance improved, and our crowds' size grew. I learned through Joe that a sensitive adviser is an effective coach.

Dr. William Cottringer's extensive survey of the primary reasons people like or dislike others supports the need for empathy. According to Cottringer, "Even the most minor and infrequent displays of rudeness greatly influence a lasting perception of unlikeability. Two of our most basic human needs are to be liked and to be successful." Each act of rudeness conveys a lack of sensitivity and counts against our total L-factor.

Empathy, however, is a powerful addition to your likeability arsenal. In fact, other people's ability to read your feelings is a key to their success with you. Ron Levant, former president of the American Psychological Association, conducted a study involving people in eighteen different countries to examine the benefits of being able to read feelings. He discovered that people of all ages who can read other people's feelings well are not only better adjusted emotionally, more outgoing, and more sensitive but also more popular.

The movie *Groundhog Day,* starring Bill Murray, is an excellent example of the difference empathy makes. Murray plays Phil Connors, a self-involved weatherman without an ounce of empathy. On assignment to cover a small-town Groundhog Day ceremony, he manages to insult every single person he meets, including his own crew.

But after a blinding snowstorm strands him in town, he awakens the next morning to find it's still February 2. And it stays February 2 day after day. At first Connors has fun in his own personal time warp, indulging in greedy, sexual, and criminal fantasies. But eventually he falls in love with his producer, Rita.

Not surprisingly, Rita rejects him. Phil then tries to win her over, and in so doing, he learns how to be a decent, likeable man. At one point he asks one of the locals, "What would you do if you were stuck in one place and everything was exactly the same and nothing that you did mattered?" The character says, "Well, that 'bout sums it up for me."

Phil's eyes open. For the first time, he empathizes with another human's condition. Slowly he develops a new perspective; he begins to see life from other people's points of view. He even participates in the community, helping people help themselves because he genuinely cares about them. These actions also help Phil win Rita's heart, and they break him out of his bizarre time warp as well.

Phil becomes likeable. Empathy does that for him. It can do it for you, too.

Like friendliness, empathy is a communication phenomenon. But these two types of communication differ sharply. When you convey friendliness, you transmit signals such as "I like you." Metaphorically speaking, you're a radio tower emitting positive vibes.

When you show empathy, however, you are more like a human satellite dish, receiving information and decoding it. You take in sights, sounds, and other signals and respond appropriately. Your ability to receive other people's signs and translate them correctly can be one of the biggest contributors to your L-factor throughout your life.

REALNESS

We're still traveling down the highway to a high L-factor, and now we encounter the final stoplight. This one asks the question: "Is this person real?"

The fact is, you can't have a high L-factor unless you possess what I call *realness*.

There are many definitions of *real*, but in the context of interpersonal relationships, I define it as "factual and actual"; in human terms, a real person is someone who is genuine, true, and authentic.

Joe Pine and Jim Gilmore, authors of *The Experience Economy*, are about to publish a new book called *Get Real*. In it they define *real* as being true to yourself and true to others; as possessing authenticity and sincerity.

"Real" people, say Pine and Gilmore, know their roots, their heritage, and their history. They remember where they came from and who brought them to the dance. And they retain that knowledge. They know their values, and they behave accordingly.

I like their definition, but no one can define the concept precisely because, at its heart, realness is something you simply feel when you're in its presence. Someone who is real to you may not seem so real to a friend.

Haven't you been in situations in which you've met someone at a party and exclaimed, "What a great person!" only to find that your spouse or friend looks at you in amazement and responds, "I thought he was a phony." No matter how you much you argue, you can't talk someone else into feeling as you do.

When you believe another person is real, you believe he or

she is sincere. What you hear is who he is. There is no veil between his true nature and your perception of it. He is the same on the outside as on the inside.

Sometimes when we search for realness in another person, we recognize it by its absence. Much like oxygen, reality becomes particularly important when it's in short supply. Few of us test every fact we hear.

After all, if we did, we'd wear ourselves out very quickly. So to some extent, we all extend a certain level of basic trust, some presumption that things are as they appear. Then, when something doesn't seem right, we snap to attention. That friendly man who empathizes with your recent financial losses and tells you that he's a great adviser seems appealing at first—until you find out he just got out of prison after serving ten years for embezzlement. At that point, you're gasping for the fresh air of a trustworthy person.

When you give others your trust, you do it not for them but for yourself. You trust people so you can get on with the details of your life.

Again, it's like breathing. You don't think about it unless you have to. Then, when you encounter someone you don't trust, the little security guard in your head snaps to attention and you wear yourself out trying to decipher the truth. This is why time flies when you're spending time with a real person, and it drags when you're forced to scrutinize all the actions of a fake.

Uncovering a fraud can be tough. In 2002 researchers brought together more than fifty of New York's finest police personnel to test their ability to detect untrue statements purely by looking at facial expressions. The detectives were shown a series of slides, each containing a picture of an accused felon along with his statement. The detectives then indicated which of the felons they believed and which ones they didn't. The researchers found that the detectives missed 98 percent of the untrue statements. Even pros can't tell sincerity just by observing the face. It takes the entire experience of interacting with someone to determine the truth.

In a powerful essay entitled "Notes on Inauthenticity and the Ring of Truth," science-fiction author and punk-rock legend John Shirley wrote, "Blunt, mindless 'honesty' does not seem to be required [when one tries to detect sincerity]–but a quality of realness does seem called for. The dictionary reference [in the definition of *sincerity*] to a matching of inward and outward character seems resonant. It is suggestive of unity, completeness [in someone's behavior]. . . . there's some quality of realness, of unadulterated genuineness, about him or her. . . . We know it when we see it, or taste it, or feel its emanation."

Let's look at three different examples of how someone's lack of realness can lower his or her L-factor.

The first is lying. When you discover that someone has lied to you, everything he or she has ever said to you is called into question. As you begin to wonder, you feel a tingling sensation crawl up the back of your neck. I call this the "you've-been-sold spider."

It's a feeling I've had several times. For example, I once hired a man based on his great qualifications and a superb interview. In six months as my employee, he charmed everyone in sight. His L-factor was as high as anyone's. Then the personnel department told me they had discovered the man had lied about his college degree. Even though the topic had never come up between us, it still made me wonder if everything he'd told me was a bill of goods. Because I liked him so much, I gave him a chance to explain himself; he told me that he was embarrassed to be a college dropout, but everything else he'd said was true. Still, I couldn't get over the lie, and I never liked him nearly as much thereafter.

A second sign of unrealness is an act of hypocrisy. One interview subject, Darcy, told a story about her yoga instructor, Shawna. Darcy loved Shawna's classes and decided she was a wonderful person as well as a wonderful teacher. Darcy loved to hear Shawna talk about how important it is to be gracious, and why we must always show respect for all living creatures.

Except waiters, apparently. When Darcy had her first meal with Shawna in a busy restaurant, the harried waiter forgot to bring Shawna her water. Shawna threw a fit, first at the apologetic waiter, then at the equally contrite manager. Darcy felt she was watching an entirely different person than the calm woman who claimed to have found balance in life. This Shawna was an unpleasant, angry, self-involved woman, and her L-factor rapidly plummeted in Darcy's eyes.

When someone is not being real with you, you feel terrible, as Darcy did. But you feel even worse if you are given praise that makes you feel great about yourself, then later find out that it was all hot air. Then you collapse like a balloon. This third type of unrealness is insincerity.

In his book *The Foundations of Personality,* prominent psychologist Abraham Myerson says, "We resent what we call 'insincerity' because we fear being fooled. . . . There is no blow quite so severe as the sudden realization that we have mistaken the opinion of others, we have been 'fooled.' To be fooled is to be lowered in one's own self-esteem, and we like sincerity and hate insincerity largely because our own self-esteem stands on some solid basis in the one case and on none whatever in the other. Most of us would rather have people say bad things of us to our face than run the risk of the ridicule and the foolish feeling that comes with insincerity."

In addition to feeling foolish, insincerity makes us feel that other people don't trust or respect us enough to tell us the truth—because they think we're too easily upset, or perhaps not intelligent enough to cope with the facts.

Interviewee Lorraine put it this way: "When someone pays me an insincere compliment or tells me what I want to hear, I feel disrespected. Clouds roll in over my impression of that person. On the other hand, when someone gets real with me, even to the point of being frank and unrestrained, I feel smart. I feel like they think I can take the truth."

Dr. William Cottringer spent several years surveying what he calls the "traits of likeability," specifically in the field of education. He says, "The reason that dishonesty and insincerity is such an important issue, leading to quick and permanent perception of unlikeability, is that we tend to personalize it. Present [insincere] behavior reminds us of a past occasion where we were deeply hurt by a person's deception. It brings this all back to us in a flash."

When we meet people who are beacons of realness, we react in the opposite manner. They make us feel good about them and about ourselves. One interviewee, Jann, talked about an old college professor who, he said, "was fortified with real. He barely managed to balance his brutal honesty with some level of sensitivity—but he did. Guys like him were resistant to all the pressures of academic life. His own ideals were always evident, and I thought he was beautiful because of it."

Another interviewee, Cindy, talked about how a lack of realness destroyed a possible relationship. Cindy met Fred through on an online dating service. She lived in San Jose; he lived in Sacramento. After two months of back-and-forth e-mail, they began a phone relationship, talked every day, and discovered they had much in common. Their passion was dogs and dog rescue.

A forty-two-year-old firefighter, Fred was thin, wore his hair short, and liked fashion. Cindy told Fred more about her life than anybody else she'd ever known.

After six months they finally decided to meet. Cindy offered to drive to Sacramento, where Fred would cook her dinner. Excited, Cindy decided to surprise him by bringing one of her dogs along.

Things didn't go well. For one thing, Fred wasn't really forty-two. He was at least fifty-five. Nor was he thin, unless you think two hundred pounds on a small frame is lean. And his hair was more than short—it was gone. Still, Cindy stayed to talk, because at least Fred was the same friendly, empathetic guy she'd talked to on the phone—except for one thing: Fred didn't seem to like her dog. Once he even "accidentally" kicked it when the pup ventured too close to his leg.

But the bottom fell out when Cindy brought up firefighting, which she had researched. Fred knew almost nothing about it. Finally he admitted that he was actually a telemarketer but had wanted to be a fireman.

"Fred was the same nice guy I met online," Cindy said. "But now I just thought his friendliness was one of his tricks. I found my way to the door in less than thirty minutes and I never looked back. He sent me the most incredibly warm follow-up e-mails to apologize, but I could never get over it."

Realness is a bedrock of culture as well as personal life. Think of Jimmy Stewart speaking up for what's right in an old Frank Capra movie, or Rocky Balboa fighting for his life in *Rocky,* or Bruce Springsteen's authentic working-class persona, or sportscaster John Madden's brutal yet boyish way of announcing football games. Realness works. We all feel a psychological need for realness because it gives us a feeling of order in our otherwise chaotic world. This is true even for culture's most recent phenomenon, reality television.

Dr. Veijo Hietala, a visiting professor of media studies at UCLA, puts it this way: "I see audiovisual popular culture . . . in particular as the mirror of the mental climate of the age and, at the same time, the therapist of its crisis. The popular genres are clearly articulating this demand for 'factual communication.' On television, it's been visual with the recent popularity of reality TV programmers. In them, the viewer specifically seeks the authentic feelings of real individuals."

To me, one of the cultural figures who best exemplifies realness is former world heavyweight boxing champion George Foreman. Currently, Foreman serves as a preacher, a leader of a Houston youth center, and a successful product endorser—in 2002 only Tiger Woods and Michael Jordan earned more in endorsement dollars.

The secret to Foreman's success is his realness-fueled likeability. Leon Dreimann, whose company bought the George Foreman grill in a nine-figure deal, recalls the first time he met Foreman, at a trade show in Las Vegas: "He was very likeable. He had an easy manner, but most of all, he didn't have this celebrity baggage at all."

The Foreman grill went on sale to fairly tepid results for a few months. Then shopping channel QVC booked Foreman to do a half-hour infomercial. Thirty minutes later the show had received more calls than any other in QVC's history. Sales skyrocketed. Dreimann watched the show over and over to figure out what had happened.

The answer? George had happened. There wasn't enough staff to answer the phones, so everyone on the set had to grab a receiver, leaving George "with nothing to do except look at hamburgers cooking on the grill, and he was hungry," says Dreimann. "So he patted his belly, took a roll, grabbed a burger, and he started eating. It was unscripted. It was completely natural. People saw that he eats what he sells."

Foreman has a "real" rule. If he doesn't like it, he won't endorse it. He became involved with the grill because he loves hamburgers, as the QVC audience witnessed.

He's also the real George Foreman at home. Though he himself is a millionaire, his small church is a humble room. He leads the congregation in a music ceremony in which he plays the guitar and sing the hymns himself.

Writer Frank Gannon recently spent several days with Foreman. He later said, "The private George Foreman isn't all that different from the public George Foreman. . . . Foreman is a real, flesh-and-blood, Home Depot–going, American man whose wife yells at him once in a while."

What works for George Foreman can work for you. Your friendliness, combined with your empathy and relevance, will make you a likeable person—but it's your ability to be real that will make you absolutely shine.

HOW TO RAISE YOUR
L-FACTOR

This chapter is designed to raise your L-factor, but it doesn't offer a onetime, one-shot, cure-all solution. Instead, you'll find here a series of small steps that will help you gradually increase your L-factor until you're more likeable than you ever imagined you could be.

Because a high L-factor is the result of skill-building and self-monitoring in a handful of areas, you will want to experiment with, refine, adjust, and repeat these exercises until you master the skills and become effortless in your high L-factor ways.

Think a better you, not a brand-new you.

Similarly, you will see results in small increments, much as you would on any intelligent new physical exercise or diet program. You don't build huge muscles in the first week; nor do you drop thirty pounds in the first month. Instead, you slowly develop new habits, new strengths, and new actions. Eventually they all add up to make a difference in your ability to generate positive thoughts, emotions, and attitudes in other people.

Remember, each of us already possesses some level of likeability. Your L-factor may be a three, a five, or an eight. But it could be higher. Following the suggestions in this book will increase it.

Keep in mind that this is not a book on the art of first impressions. I offer you no tips on can't-fail pick-up lines or short-term strategies guaranteed to turn strangers into temporary friends. While a first impression is important, it won't carry a long-term relationship.

You must raise your L-factor in a sustainable way. You want people to continue to like you over time. You want a high L-factor that won't quit.

So how do you raise your L-factor?

You raise it by improving the four elements of likeability: friendliness, relevance, empathy, and realness.

Before beginning, though, consider a few pieces of advice.

• Some of these exercises will make immediate sense to you. Underline them. They are the low-hanging fruit to pick from this book and will improve your life right away. Try to implement them quickly.

• Other exercises may seem odd. Place a question mark in the margin next to each one. Ask yourself if the exercise is truly unusual or just new to you. Perhaps it's an exercise you simply don't want to do. Before you reject it, think it over. But if an exercise truly is a glaring contradiction to who you are and what you value, forget it. Never fake any part of being likeable.

• Measure the ease with which you implement each exercise. If a skill comes easily, you've got a natural tendency to do it well. Pay attention to these points because you can use them right away.

• Imagine that someone you know and respect is watching

you. Would he or she be proud or puzzled as you implement these techniques? Would he or she say, "I knew you had it in you"? Or "Wait a minute, this isn't really you"? Maintaining such a perspective will help you maintain your realness.

One of the best ways to determine which L-factor techniques come most naturally to you is to complete the Finding Your Likeable Self exercise.

FINDING YOUR LIKEABLE SELF

Do you remember the 1980s New Wave classic song "What I Like About You," by the Romantics? One of the features the singer liked was that "you really know how to dance." Another was that "[you] tell me all the things that I wanna to hear." Those lyrics provide some examples of high L-factor features observed in the person about whom the Romantics were singing.

Now imagine they're singing that song just to you, and listing all your likeable features.

Think about the features people like about you. They might include anything from a physical attribute, like a winning smile, to a constant practice, such as complimenting others, or even an odd fact, such as the way you get along with animals. These features will form the foundation for your future, higher L-factor self. (And don't be modest here—no one will read your list except you. If people think you have great eyes, say so. Anyway, if you hear it often, it's probably true.)

Take out a small notebook, which will become your personal L-factor journal. (I prefer a leather journal because it lasts longer, but any journal will do. Make sure to carry a pen or pencil with you at all times, because you never know when inspiration will strike. You'll also need a yellow highlighter and a green highlighter.)

Start out on a fresh page and write the following header at the top: "My L-factor Features."

Ready? Now write down your responses to the following.

1. *Try to recall the last time someone paid you a compliment.* It could have happened anytime—at home, at work, at the mall. Recollect the day, the time, the words used, and what you were doing at that moment. Write down the compliment, what you did to inspire it, and the frequency with which you hear this particular compliment ("rarely," "occasionally," or "often").

2. *Look back over the past year and select the compliment you most enjoyed receiving.* This compliment is consistent with your best sense of yourself. For example, if you've been working hard to sharpen your sense of humor and last month your boss said you were funny, write the compliment down, along with what you did to inspire it.

3. *Think about your biggest fan.* Don't use a family member; choose someone who doesn't feel obligated to say nice things about you. This person talks about you in glowing terms to others. Write down his or her name in your journal. What converted him or her from an acquaintance to a supporter? Was it one thing you did, or a series of events? Write it down. If he or she were to list your two most likeable features, what would they be? Write them down.

4. *What would be your response if you were asked in a job interview to name your best quality?* Write it down.

5. *Except for your spouse or partner, pick any family member who has* *a positive attitude about you.* Which of your features would he or she rate as your most appealing? Write down both the person's name and the favorite feature. If you're drawing a blank, try this: If he or she were describing you to a potential mate, employer, or partner, what would he or she say were your major selling points?

6. *Consider either your best friend or your significant other.* If he or she listed your top two features, what would they be? To jog your memory, think of the trait about which he or she most often compliments you. Write down the compliments and the features that inspire them.

Perhaps you've been writing down the same features in answer to several questions. These features represent a pattern of high L-factor behaviors.

7. *Think of a role model—someone you admire and want to emulate.* He or she can be a current celebrity, a historical figure, or someone you actually know. The key is that this person possesses features you'd like to have. Write down his or her name and top two appealing features.

8. *Pick one day-to-day influence in your life.* He or she might be a friend, a family member, a boss, an acquaintance—but not your role model. This is a person whose mannerisms you find yourself adopting, on purpose or by accident. He or she came up with a new phrase that you started using a week later, or has a particular work-related habit that you've borrowed. His or her influence may come from your constant contact, or because you find yourself attracted to the way he or she thinks. Write down this person's name and the two features you like most.

You have now written down eight responses. Reread them every few weeks. Some of my seminar attendees have taken these features directly into other parts of their lives and expanded them, seeing an immediate lift in their L-factor—even before they heard new advice and techniques!

(For example, in response to question 6, one attendee found that her significant other thought her ability to listen well was her most likeable feature, so she immediately decided to take her great set of ears to work. Although she knew she listened closely to her partner, she realized that she didn't pay as much attention to her coworkers. She started doing so—and found that that they were delighted.)

But for now, identify the features that contribute to a high L-factor in yourself and others. For example, review your answer to question 1. If one of the last compliments you received was that you're a good listener, locate the keyword in that statement and circle the word "listener" in your journal. For question 6, if your wife said your most endearing feature is your candor, circle the word "candor."

Of all the circled words, pay the most attention to those for numbers 2 (your favorite compliment over the past year) and 7 (the features of your role model). These are the features you cherish in yourself as well as observe in someone you admire. Highlight these in yellow so they jump off the page.

Now look for features that you may or may not have thought about prior to this exercise. These traits may be a surprise. They are your newly discovered features, ones you should consider integrating into your life. Highlight these in light green.

Across the top of a new page, write "My Greatest L-factor Hits." Write down the top five features you've identified during this exercise, describing either yourself or other people. At the top of your list would be the features that came up over and over again, or the ones you particularly value. These are your natural L-factor talents.

|||

Congratulations! You've just pinpointed several important attributes to develop as you embark on your likeability training. Finding your likeable self is a bold first step on your way to a higher L-factor.

Now you must dig in and learn new ways to develop the winning qualities of friendliness, relevance, empathy, and realness. There are three major steps to achieving success in each category. We'll observe them one by one.

Here come a dozen bits of high-performance L-factor fuel!

FRIENDLINESS

1. Observe No Unfriendliness
2. Develop a Friendly Mind-set
3. Communicate Friendliness

To be likeable, first and foremost you must be friendly. As simple as that sounds, friendliness is not the norm. The world is filled with unfriendliness, because being friendly requires time, attention, and mental focus. But anyone and everyone can improve their friendliness quotient if they're willing to try. The following discussion will show you how to think, act, and feel differently—and I bet you'll see the results more quickly than you might expect.

1. Observe No Unfriendliness

Perhaps the best way to boost your friendliness is to eliminate unfriendliness from your behavior.

Because so many people are accustomed to being treated in an unfriendly fashion, the mere absence of unfriendliness can be perceived as friendliness. So simply getting rid of unfriendly behavior is a wonderful start.

Your first action in the friendliness program will be to go on a strict no-unfriendliness diet. Treat unfriendliness as someone with diabetes treats sugar. Starting right now, adopt a policy of zero tolerance for being unfriendly.

How will you observe this new policy? The same way you avoid any breakdown: prevention, intervention, and repair.

First, practice the *prevention* of unfriendliness by adopting a new perspective. A perspective shift happens when you see the world in a new way, resulting in new rules, values, and realities.

Think of your perspective as your operating system. It determines your reactions and your reflexes. A new perspective will yield new reactions and reflexes.

Tom, a young resident at a midwestern hospital whom I met while giving a seminar, had just such a paradigm shift. Tom had been using unfriendliness—banging clipboards, snarling at nurses, and yelling at patients—to get what he wanted. Then one day the hospital supervisors took Tom aside and informed him that his negative approach wasn't helpful in retaining nurses, raising the morale of the department, or maintaining quality in patient health care. They told him he was on probation.

Tom is a smart man. Realizing he was in serious trouble, he shifted his perspective by installing two thoughts in his mind:

1. *Unfriendliness is a weakness.* Every time you're unfriendly with someone, you've experienced a failure to control yourself.

2. *Friendliness is a strength.* When you've been friendly, you've been strong. You've flexed your friendliness muscles. Challenge yourself to maintain friendliness despite the stimuli around you. Don't succumb to the weakness of unfriendliness. Make it a matter of pride.

I want you to install these same thoughts. And don't make this shift a secret, either. Go public with the new you. A new attitude needs a bit of advertising. Share your thoughts with friends and family. Make a lively discussion out of it. Post a sign in your cubicle. Put a sticky note on your mirror.

One seminar attendee took a very creative approach. He created a vanity license plate with the letters I-O-N-U: I Observe No Unfriendliness.

| | |

The second step in the unfriendliness-elimination program is *intervention.* Intervene to catch yourself before you commit unfriendliness, using the following techniques.

- Practice spotting unfriendliness bubbling up inside you before it emerges. Although individual emotional systems differ, we all experience general warning signs. You might notice a bad feeling right before you act unfriendly, such as an ache in your head or a pit in your stomach. You might start shaking, or sense blood rushing to your face. Each of us has our own individual way of knowing that we're about to erupt. Once you actively look for these signals, you'll gradually improve your ability to spot them—with luck, before you've lost control and committed yourself to an unfriendly reaction.

• When you sense yourself about to commit an unfriendly act, talk yourself out of it by asking yourself two questions and making two statements. They won't all apply at the same time, but at least one of them should work.

  • Will this fix anything?
  • Is this how I want to be remembered?
  • You are welcome here.
  • I should be helping you.

These four interventions can help you collect yourself, regain your perspective, and stop an unfriendly act before it happens. Many seminar attendees report that they seldom get past the first one—the answer is usually no, and the fire of unfriendliness is extinguished on the spot.

DEALING WITH ANGER

It's one thing to have an unfriendly feeling coming on. It's another to feel very angry with someone. If that's the case, here's some advice on how to deal with it.

A display of extreme anger can be the loudest dose of unfriendliness you'll ever give someone, which is why the subject of anger management has inspired countless books, treatment programs, and even movies. Here's a short course on anger management.

• *Delay your anger gratification.* You may be conditioned to believe that telling someone off on the spot will give you a sense of satisfaction and relief, or to think it will feel good to know you're not bottling up your anger. Instead, postpone your response. Put it off one day. As you do, contemplate what would truly make you feel better. After all, venting your anger often doesn't really make you feel good in the long run because it leaves a trail of unhappiness behind you. (Remember me and my friend Curtis?)

• *Reframe the situation.* Attempt to recast the person you're angry with in a different light. Perhaps he or she wasn't the cause of your anger but simply the messenger. Ask yourself: Is this person really the reason for my anger? Does this person truly mean me ill? Will yelling at this person improve the situation? Reframing can reduce the emotional content in a situation and quell your angry feelings. You may even be able to focus on a positive, constructive solution.

• *Commit to acknowledging no anger and no unfriendliness aloud.* When you feel anger coming on, speak intelligently. Say things like "I do not want to be angry with you. Can you help me?" This effective intervention can defuse otherwise explosive situations.

• *Cordially remove yourself from the situation.* Pretend you're a diplomat. Don't show your hand. Leave so you can regroup and control yourself. You don't have to hang up the phone or slam a door. Instead, pleasantly find a way to end the current conversation and politely excuse yourself.

• *If you do need to vent your anger, do it in private, or with a trusted friend.* Yelling at the person you feel is responsible for your anger has no special medicinal or psychological value. Go to the gym and take it out on a set of weights or a punching bag. That punching bag won't lower your L-factor; only people can do that.

• *Even if you can't control your anger, it's not over.* Setbacks can provide lessons. Get back on the horse. You're not necessarily unfriendly. You just screwed up once. Think of it this way: Each time you succumb to being unfriendly, you gain more insight into spotting the unfriendliness bubbling within. You'll also discover which of the above techniques works best for you.

Every time you catch yourself being unfriendly, write an account of it on a fresh page in your journal. Answer these questions: Who made you feel mad? What happened? When did it happen? What provoked you? How were you feeling?

Whenever you have to return to your journal to log a new bout of unfriendliness, review your previous notes. These reviews will sharpen your skills and help you to improve your perspective.

| | |

The third thing you must do to eliminate unfriendliness is *repair*. When you have a setback and act unfriendly, you must repair the damage.

Apologize. Yes, this can be difficult, especially when you feel you've been wronged. I'm not suggesting that you forgive people for everything they do. Just realize that unfriendliness is hurtful whatever its cause and be sorry for yours.

As soon as you can, express your personal regret in words to the person you blew up at. Be honest and say how you feel. People can deny or dispute the facts but not feelings. By telling others how you feel, you open up the door to a constructive conversation that can enhance others' perception of your friendliness.

Together, prevention, intervention, and repair can reengineer the way you approach other people.

2. Develop a Friendly Mind-set

Before you study the behaviors that communicate friendliness, you first need to make sure your attitude is friendly. To do that, you must develop a way of thinking in which friendliness is the default position.

Following are ten different ways to create and maintain a friendly mind-set. As you read, pick those that work best for you, and discard those that don't. (Again, always keep it real—do what makes sense for the real you.)

1. *Like yourself.* You have to believe you deserve a high L-factor in order to have one. The good news is that you've already done a lot of work toward this end. If you take out your journal and review the Finding Your Likeable Self exercise, you'll notice many of your most endearing features in the responses to numbers 3, 4, 5, and 6. Memorize them. Name these traits aloud. Realize that they are an intrinsic part of you. As you establish friendliness toward yourself, you'll find you are friendlier toward others, too.

2. *See yourself in others.* When you spot your favorite traits in other people, you're likely to be friendly to them. Learn to recognize your likeable traits as they appear in others. It's like playing the license-plate game on a long car trip: "I spotted Texas!" "There goes Rhode Island!" Similarly, you can say to yourself, "She's got a great sense of humor," or "There goes a really honest person."

3. *Review your role model's best features.* Reread your journal entry "My Greatest L-factor Hits." Review the responses to number 7. There you noted two features you admired in another person. Now take a few minutes and find two more. Then spot those features in strangers, coworkers, and friends. The more of these traits you find, the more likely you are to establish friendly attitudes toward the people who possess them.

4. *Recast everyone you meet as the solution to today's problem.* When someone is a solution to what you need, you're inclined to like them. Think of yourself as a casting director in the movie called *My Life Today,* and look for people to cast in the role of Helpful Friend.

For example, if you're trying to find the location of your noon meeting, when someone walks in the door, envision that person as the one who knows exactly where you need to be. It will change the way you see him or her. As you develop this bias, you will be surprised to find out how frequently other people possess your solution for the day.

5. *Apply your fundamental beliefs.* Whether political, spiritual, or religious, employ all the wonderful concepts you've learned throughout your life about why you should help others, why people are precious, and why you should cherish them.

6. *Play greeter for a day.* Think of a department store greeter, or your favorite maître d' at a friendly restaurant. Emulate this person for a day. Open the door for someone carrying a large suitcase. Let someone else walk in front of you through a room. Take it upon yourself to instill a sense of welcome in others. You will receive positive feedback as well as good feelings that will make this a job you'd like to have all the time.

7. *Top your best service every week.* Recall a time when you helped someone in some important way. Take out your journal and on a new page write "My Best Service." Underneath it describe the specifics of that situation and how it made you feel, as well as how it made your friend feel. Leave a couple of blank pages here because, for the next six Fridays, I want you to challenge yourself to find a new service best and document it.

At the end of six weeks, read the pages you've filled with your progressive efforts at being able to better serve others. You may notice a pattern that will make it easier for you to understand your best service talents.

8. *Study the helpful.* Find people in the course of your everyday life who are supportive. These people tend to be very receptive, so they might agree if you asked to interview them about how and why they do it.

Ask questions such as these: How do you always manage to be so helpful? Why do you do this? Why do you do it so often? How has it affected your life?

You will be surprised at the stories you hear of delight, reciprocation, and friendship. Review these interviews over time to learn not just how it's done but, more important, how these people built their friendly mind-set and how they constantly refuel it through use.

9. *Every morning repeat your friendliness mantras as you prepare for or drive to work.* These are statements you say or chant to yourself to help shape your attitude. You might say, "People are welcome in my world," "I like you," or "My friendliness is how I make a difference." Repeat these a few times every morning to set a positive tone for the rest of your day.

Add new mantras to your repertoire every few months so they don't grow stale. For inspiration, look at self-help books in your library or a bookstore. Remember to choose a statement that involves positive feelings toward others.

10. *Protect your friendly mind-set.* One of the toughest obstacles to maintaining your friendliness is the contagious nature of unfriendliness coming from other people. Dr. Norman Vincent Peale, author of *The Power of Positive Thinking*, once said that we must expel all negative people from our lives because their attitudes are toxic. I agree. Learn to weed out the unfriendly. You may have to change your patterns in small ways, avoiding certain places or social activities. But you must defend your friendly mind-set as though you were protecting a most valuable asset.

All together, if you practice some or all of these ten habits every day, you will create a mind-set that leaves out only the how: "How do I communicate my friendliness?"

3. Communicate Friendliness

Armed with friendly thoughts, you are now prepared to boost your friendliness factor.

The trick to being friendlier is to remember that there is no such thing as a friendly person per se. There is only someone who is perceived as friendly by others.

Friendliness is a communication event. If other people don't perceive you as friendly, you aren't friendly.

People decode your messages and determine that you are friendly by picking up on the cues you send. Those cues are delivered by various means, some more important than others.

Dr. Albert Mehrabian, a communications researcher at the University of California, Los Angeles, is renowned for his pioneering work in the field of nonverbal communication. One of his main theories is that people always supply clues as to their intentions. Others, in turn, decode what people say based on these visual and auditory clues, as well as the actual words being spoken.

Based on extensive experiments dealing with the communication of feelings and the attitudes of like/dislike, Dr. Mehrabian concluded that 55 percent of the like/dislike cues people give are visual, mostly facial. Thirty-eight percent of the cues are transmitted via tone of voice. And the remaining 7 percent are verbal (the actual words used).

Dr. Mehrabian, who reported the results of his research in the book *Silent Messages,* concluded that when we send mixed signals to people, they believe what they see (or perceive) more than what is actually said.

In this section you will learn methods to improve your visual, auditory, and verbal friendliness communication skills.

Your first and most important task is to send the right visual signals to others in order to communicate your friendly intentions and positive feelings.

SHOW FRIENDLY SIGNS

Let's start with your face.

First, consider your eyes. Always highly expressive, they can communicate your attitude, your energy level, and much more. To maintain friendly eyes:

- *Make eye contact.* If you look away from others in conversation, they'll perceive you as unfriendly. When you make direct eye contact, you show you're engaged, open, and responsive.
- *Don't overdo the eye contact.* Too much can turn into a stare-down. That can seem intimidating, or just weird.
- *Use your eyebrows.* Let them dance along with your voice and the thoughts you're trying to convey. The more animated your eyebrows, the more outgoing, engaged, and friendly

you'll seem. The best way to express a positive thought is to raise your eyebrows; your entire face lifts when you raise your eyebrows, as if to say, "I am open for you." To communicate a negative thought, furrow or lower them.

• *Use your eyes to show emotion.* Widen your eyes for interest or passion. This will signal that you are reacting (and welcoming) what others are saying. When you narrow your eyes, you send the signal that you either don't believe or don't agree.

Now let's move down a few inches, to the mouth. Here the key is your smile. A smile is the most effective of all the visual cues that communicate friendliness; it is a substantial contributor to your friendliness factor.

Dr. Robert S. Feldman, professor of psychology at the University of Massachusetts, Amherst, conducted research in the 1990s that found that the percentage of time you smile during a conversation has a direct bearing on your perceived friendliness. The more, the friendlier.

To smile more often and more effectively:

• *Keep your smile real.* Don't force it. A genuine smile is the only effective and friendly smile.

• *Study great smiles.* Don't copy them; reverse engineer them. That is, identify great smiles in friends, family, and celebrities, and then look into the smilers' minds. Ask yourself where the smile originates and how it happens. If you know these people well, ask them why they smile. The conversation may lead you to great discoveries. By studying others' smiles, you can unlock the secrets to your own smiling process.

• *Look through your photos to find your own best smiles.*

Study your childhood photos, yearbook pictures, and recent snapshots. Examine this collection, and identify the genuine, warm, and wonderful smiles you've displayed. Think about the thoughts and feelings you had at those times, and how those smiles made other people feel. In your journal, at the top of a page, write "My Top Ten Smiles." List your smiles from your favorite on down. Next to them list when they occurred, who the recipient was, and how you felt. Return to this list every time you want some understanding about when and where you smile best.

• *Recall your smiling compliments.* Return to your journal and write the heading "Been Caught Smiling." Under it list compliments you've received related to your smile. Review the Finding Your Likeable Self exercise to see if any of the people in your life like you because you have a great smile. If so, you're in luck. You already have a winning smile. Otherwise, from this point forward, note the reactions to the new, smiling you. The more you smile, the more you will hear things like "You have a great smile." Really! Try this for six weeks. Then go back and read every compliment aloud and recollect the details. This repetitive exercise will reinforce the value of smiling and put you in a positive feedback loop that can lead to a constant state of smiling, as well as perceived friendliness.

• *Combine your expressive eyes with your winning smile.* A smile communicates friendliness, but when combined with expressive eyes, it produces a synergy that can't be beat. These two features together will equal more perceived friendliness than either one alone.

• *Smile at anyone, anytime you feel it.* You don't need permission. Many people limit their smiles to if/then conditions: *If* someone does X, *then* you smile. Some of us have set a very high bar on what it takes to make us smile. Get over it. Lower the bar to the floor.

• *Invest in a confident smile.* Perhaps you don't smile as much as you could because you're self-conscious about your teeth. Maybe they're not as white as you would like. Buy whitening strips, or ask your dentist to do the job. You'll notice a desire to show off your pearly smile. The same is true with dental work you might be putting off. Invest in your future smile confidence. You don't need perfect teeth to have a great smile. You do need confidence to display that smile often.

• *When you greet others, lead with your smile.* Let them see your smile before they hear your voice or your words. Think of your smile as your first foot forward.

Moving down to the rest of your body, here's some advice on friendly body language.

• *Hold your head up when you talk.* It shows a level of engagement and is perceived as warm and friendly.

• *Maintain good posture.* It demonstrates interest as well as openness. Slouching is perceived as unfriendly because it indicates disengagement.

• *Display openness.* Always think open, not closed, when it comes to your body. Imagine yourself as an opening flower, not a closing door. Let this mental picture guide all of your body language. Limit the crossing of arms. They can signal a closed mind.

• *Don't tap your feet while someone talks to you.* Relaxed feet are friendlier than nervous, tapping feet. Relaxation shows that you are interested and have the time to listen to someone. Tapping says, "Hurry up, I'm losing interest."

All together, these different visual cues can combine to send the powerful message that you like someone and you're happy to see them.

MAKE FRIENDLY SOUNDS

You can also improve the sounds you make—not only your tone and voice but also the overall auditory experience you provide to others.

- *Silence can be unfriendly.* Words break the ice. You may remember a situation in which you were sitting next to a stranger on a train or plane, and you found him or her mildly irritating in some way. It made you want to do something unfriendly. Maybe you did. Next time, speak. Start a conversation. When you begin to talk, you can form a connection that may dissolve your irritation. Maybe the person isn't as irksome as you thought, and you will discover how interesting he or she is. At worst, he or she may end up being as unpleasant as you first perceived. When that happens, and I believe it is rare, at least you know for sure.

- *Record yourself speaking, then listen to the tape.* At first you may hate the sound of your voice, but you'll get over that, and by listening to it and studying it, you may improve it. Eventually you'll sense whether your tone is friendly or unfriendly. (Caveat: Never invade someone's privacy when you record yourself. Use a handheld recorder to record only your side of a phone conversation, or simply review the outgoing messages you've set up at work or on your cell phone.)

- *Study people with friendly voices.* We all know others

whose vocal tones make us feel warm and positive. By hearing and studying these voices, you'll be able to adopt them in your day-to-day conversations.

• *Avoid raising your voice whenever possible.* Loud is usually equated with unfriendly. Reduce the required volume of a statement by a notch. Practice the art of soft undertones—they are perceived as warmer and friendlier.

• *Don't match tones with other people when they are unfriendly, upset, or angry.* Maintain your friendly, calm tone, even in the face of severe negativity.

• *Listen to yourself in conversation for tone violations.* When they happen, stop the conversation, share your feelings, and start over. If someone says, "Don't use that tone of voice with me," a warning bell should go off, and you should consider pausing the conversation to express how you feel without the negative tone.

• *Add variety to your speaking voice.* Make it dynamic. Go up, go down; show a range of inflection. These modulations indicate that you're engaged and communicate a high energy level, which in turn drives the perception that you're a friendly person.

• *Speak in a confident tone.* Confidence says, "I trust you," "I like you," and "I believe in myself." It signals warmth and friendliness.

USE FRIENDLY WORDS

Your verbal content may constitute only 7 percent of your cues in others' minds. But those words can live forever and can make all the difference in whether or not others perceive you as friendly.

For example, a person's name is the friendliest word in the world to his or her ears. Make a habit of learning names and using them. If, like many people, you have trouble remembering names, repeat the name and form a mental association with it. For example, if you met me, you could say "Tim" (and then think "Tiny Tim") and "Sanders" (and think "Colonel Sanders"). Now your mind can conjure up a toy-sized Colonel Sanders when I appear.

Don't overuse a person's name, however. Too much repetition becomes both corny and condescending.

Friendly words ultimately convey your liking, your helpfulness, and your openness to another person. Examples of words that convey liking or a positive attitude toward someone include *love, wonderful, excellent, magnificent, awesome, beautiful, perfect, inspiring,* and *appreciate.*

Words or phrases that convey welcome or openness include *yes, welcome, nice to see you, glad you are here,* and *come in.*

Words or phrases that display a sense of helpfulness include *how can I help? what can I do? gladly, with pleasure, absolutely,* and *sure.*

These are just a few examples; you get the picture. But none of them will be effective if expressed in a negative tone of voice. A positive tone needs to accompany these words if you wish to convey friendliness.

In contrast, some unfriendly words and phrases include *go away, can't, won't, I'm busy, not today, some other time, ask someone else, do I have to?, stop, hate, not my job, never, unwelcome* . . . and any profanity.

The word *no,* especially as the first word in a sentence, can be very unfriendly. *Hate* is always an unfriendly word; avoid it. Using insulting words such as *fat, awful,* and *stupid* to describe a negative feeling about another person also position you as unfriendly overall.

Generalizations, such as *you always do* and *you never do,* can also make you seem unfriendly. If you must make a valid criticism, do it without making it seem as though the other person is incapable of correcting it. Be specific.

Note: The words *please* and *thanks* are neutral words; depending on their inflection and their context, they can either be friendly or unfriendly. "Can you please do this?" barked in an impolite tone can sound like a command or a sarcastic remark. Likewise, if you add *thanks* at the end of a passive-aggressive statement or an insult, it's even more biting. ("Could you please be a little less of an idiot next time? Thanks.") So watch your use of such words.

E-mail is a terrible medium in which to communicate feelings because it lacks appropriate nonverbal cues. E-mails often come across as curt statements, making the recipient's blood boil.

Let's say a friend sends you a long e-mail, explaining her frustration with her relationship. You reply via e-mail from your handheld pager, "Bummer. Hope it works out. Later." You're sympathetic, but you're in a hurry and you find it hard to type long messages on the tiny keyboard. Your friend now finds you insensitive. But if you were talking face-to-face, you'd make eye contact and display your sympathy through your tone of voice and body language

If, in retrospect, you feel that you've sent someone an unfriendly e-mail, pick up the phone and find out if your hunch is correct. Your intervention may well avoid an incident of perceived unfriendliness that could be forwarded via e-mail to the entire world, or stored on someone's hard drive for years.

One final note: Never take your perceived friendliness for granted. Just because you sent out friendly signals last time you saw someone doesn't mean that you're communicating friendliness every time. Your assigned friendliness factor, much like your L-factor, is always subject to change. So watch yourself, and watch your cues. Your friendliness factor is fragile.

RELEVANCE

1. Identify your Frequent Contact Circle
2. Connect with Others' Interests
3. Connect with Others' Wants and Needs

Raising your relevance factor is a wonderful complement to your newfound friendliness.

As noted, being relevant means having a connection to others' everyday interests, wants, or needs. You'll need relevance to have a high L-factor. Some of us may be wasting our time trying to raise our L-factor with people with whom we have no connection. Remember, to whom you matter is just as important as who matters to you. Fish where the fish are biting. Know where you're relevant, and cast your line there.

In this section you'll learn how to identify others who find you relevant and how to develop relevance with others.

1. Identify Your Frequent Contact Circle

Previously you learned that when others are in constant contact with you, they have a bias to like you.

The next exercise will help you find these people. Flip to a new page in your journal and write "My Frequent Contact Circle" across the top of a new page. Here you will list the names of everyone you are in contact with on at least a monthly basis, without any order or priority, one to a line.

Think carefully about this task. Take as much time as you want and use as many pages as you need.

Most people start with the easy ones, such as family members, friends, and coworkers, but don't forget to write down people with whom you might serve on a committee, a nonprofit group, or a sports team. Also remember the people with whom you interact because of your kids or pets or medical needs. List your day-to-day service providers. Think about the dry cleaner, the doorman, the produce manager at the grocery store. All of them may be in your frequent contact circle.

At this point you may have several pages filled with the names of people you see every month. It's time to rate each contact for quality. To do this, identify the frequency and the proximity of your contact with each of them.

By frequency, I mean how often you have contact with them—for example, every day.

By proximity, I mean whether you see them on a face-to-face basis.

Take a look at your list and give each contact an approximate rating on a scale of one to ten. For example, the family member you see every day is a ten. The distant friend with whom you exchange e-mail once a month is a one.

After you've gone through this scoring exercise, reread your list. You'll see a series of tens, nines, and eights. These are your most frequent, close-proximity contacts. On a new piece of paper, write "My Top Contacts." Then write down each of these names on a separate line, allowing two spaces beneath each one, for up to twenty names. You'll return to this list later.

You have now a list of your top contacts based on frequency and proximity. This is your prospect list for high L-factor connections. You are highly relevant to these people because you are in close and frequent contact with them, making them likely to be receptive to your efforts to boost your L-factor.

This list is important because it can help you prioritize your L-factor efforts. Successful salespeople have hot-prospects lists that enable them to focus on their most likely customers, saving them time and energy. Your own list represents those people who are most likely to respond to your friendliness, empathy, and realness.

One seminar attendee, in talking about the list, quoted an old sales strategy: "If you want to catch a few fish, don't start by trying to boil the ocean."

You might want to revisit your list every time you're trying to find a way to boost your L-factor. It will also come in handy later, because in future exercises you'll need to know your frequent contacts' interests and needs.

INCREASE THE QUALITY AND QUANTITY OF YOUR CONTACTS

Some of you may have a list that's high on quantity but low on quality. That is, you may have e-mail correspondences with hundreds of people but find few of them relevant because you don't have quality contact with them.

But you can increase the quality of your frequent contact circle.

Warm up your channel of communication. For the most part, we tend to have contact with other people in defined routines: in daily face-to-face meetings, in once-a-week phone calls, or through regular e-mail. Each of these examples is a different communication channel—facial, vocal, digital.

Keep in mind that the digital channel, e-mail, is the coldest form of communication. It sends the fewest cues, communicates the fewest emotions, and produces the lowest-quality contact. You will seldom be relevant to someone if all your contact is through e-mail.

If you have many e-mail relationships (those people on your list who rank as ones, twos, or threes), find a way to pick up the phone once a week, or at the very least once a month, and have a conversation. Even if they live halfway across the world, it is not only affordable but desirable to shift the communication from e-mail to voice to improve the quality of your contact.

The telephone is a far better vehicle to create some warmth in your communication. You can establish relevance through happiness, laughter, sadness, and all the other voice-expressed emotions. Many people are able to preserve long-distance relationships through voice contact alone. But both of you must be committed over the long haul; it's hard to maintain a phone-only relationship.

The best relationship is a face-to-face one.

If someone with whom you normally talk on the phone is convenient to see, make it happen. Have a party. Meet for coffee. Upgrade the channel of communication. The warmer, the better.

After reflecting on this exercise, you may decide that you'd like to increase the number of people you see. Maybe you don't even have a top-ten list at this point. The best way to increase the number of your frequent contacts is to decrease the amount of time you spend alone.

There are many times in your life when you need to be alone. At other times you choose to be alone. And there are times when you're alone only because you've been too lazy to make other arrangements. These latter moments present excellent opportunities to seek out real contact with others.

If you drive to work solo, consider car pooling. Many organizations offer a car-pool list, making it simple to sign up. You'll immediately add two, three, or four frequent contacts to your list.

Play games with real people instead of the computer. Many of us privatize our entertainment by playing in front of our terminal when we could be having fun with our family and friends. Find a way to move your pastimes from private to public.

Stop eating lunch alone. It's easy to get into this habit, but easy to break out of it, too. Introduce yourself to your neighbor who always eats at the same lunch stand you do. Join the table at work where you see peers. Say hello to the stranger at the counter who's always there when you are.

Get out in the world. Many of us now shop online. Try visiting a store sometime. It's not only fun but also provides an opportunity to meet people along the way. Look for new clubs and organizations to join. Search for things that interest you and become a part of them, whether a nonprofit organization, a hobby group, or a workout class.

After completing this exercise, many of my seminar attendees are amazed at how little attention they've devoted to their top-ten contacts. Instead, they've been spending their life fishing fruitlessly for a higher L-factor from people with whom they have little or no contact.

If you have some kind of contact, it can be the basis for relevance at its most fundamental—you're a part of the fabric of someone else's life.

2. Connect with Others' Interests

When you share an interest with others, you develop a bond. This bond will boost your relevance factor, giving you a higher L-factor.

To start, create an inventory of your passions.

Assess your own current interests. Review and reflect on your pastimes, your hobbies, and your passions. If you don't have a handle on what you care about, how can you develop mutual interests with others?

I usually refer to interests and hobbies as passions because most people are more passionate about them than about their work. Thus likeability and interests are related, because when two people have a passion in common, they are connected at the sweet spot, which is at the heart of being relevant.

On a fresh piece of paper in your journal, write the header "My Stash of Passions." Now list your favorite activities outside of work, leaving two blank lines beneath each one. Examples include exercise, music, politics, attending ball games, visiting art galleries, doing yoga, and shopping. Don't forget your hobbies, such as collecting stamps or antiques, and projects you enjoy, such as model-building or home improvement.

After you've listed all of your passions, under each one write the names of friends and acquaintances who share these passions. Then, returning to the list one more time, write down one of your current acquaintances whom you suspect might also enjoy this activity.

Think hard. Be creative. Consider what other people like, and whether or not a bridge can be built between their interests and your passions.

This exercise will help you boost your relevance factor with others, because:

• *You have to be aware of your interests in order to share them.* You may have forgotten some of these interests, or perhaps they've been a part of your life for so long, you no longer think of them as passions but as part of your everyday routine. Or maybe you'll dust off an old activity or hobby and take it up again. This inventory may help you remember your interests so you can discuss them in social situations; you're likely to make connections more quickly and develop relevance faster.

• *People in your life will find you relevant once you start talking about your shared interests.* For example, after finishing this exercise, seminar attendee Rich realized that he and his boss were both enthused about dieting. Previously, Rich had felt he had little in common with his boss, but once Rich realized they were both counting calories and carbs, he started to share advice and pointers with the man. Eventually the boss adopted Rich as his unofficial diet guru, calling him from food stores to ask his opinion about prospective purchases. Rich's relevance factor with his boss soared accordingly.

Through this exercise you may well find one of these sleeping connections in your life. All you need to do is wake it up and get going.

Alex, another seminar attendee, made a connection between his passion for flying radio-controlled airplanes and his brother-in-law's love for building model airplanes. He reasoned that since they both loved (small) planes, his brother-in-law, with whom Alex felt he had little in common, might enjoy flying them in the park. Alex made the call. Now the two get together almost every weekend.

After completing this exercise, some people realize they have only a few interests and passions. This is not uncommon. Maybe you're in a rut. Maybe you've been working so hard in your fast-paced life, you haven't left yourself time for a passion. Remember the old saying "The only difference between a rut and a grave is the depth." Perhaps it's time to develop new interests (or rekindle old ones) so you have a base from which to bond with others.

For those who are determined to find more interests, here are a few things you can do.

• *Rediscover an old passion.* This might be an activity or a hobby that didn't make your list because you haven't thought about it in years. Review your list and consider what didn't make the cut that could have. Revisit this passion—whether it's bicycling or movies or art.

• *Do some research.* Go to a bookstore, nose around the magazine rack, and ask questions. Publications exist for almost every hobby and interest imaginable; thumb through these magazines. Something might jump off the page and become your next big passion. It may already have a huge network of fans in your life, giving your relevance factor a needed boost.

• *Ask your best friend or significant other what he or she thinks you might enjoy.* He or she may suggest you look into something you hadn't considered, like sailing, coin collecting, or even adopting a pet.

IDENTIFY THE INTERESTS OF YOUR MOST FREQUENT CONTACTS

Now reverse your perspective. Instead of thinking about your interests, think about others'. In this exercise, you will identify others' passions and try some of them on for size or, at least, develop some curiosity about them.

Return to your "My Top Contacts" list. You know these people well; it's time for you to leverage that knowledge.

When making the list, you left a few blank lines beneath each name. On the first empty line, write the word "Passions," followed by a colon, then one activity or hobby this person enjoys.

If you wish, expand your thinking to include anything your frequent contact enthuses over, whether it's cats, an alma mater, or cable television.

When you finish, you'll notice the pattern of various interests among your frequent contacts. Review the entire list. Circle at least three activities that you yourself might enjoy. Perhaps you've already thought about them. If so, you'll find an easy connection between a friend's existing interest and you. Say something. Your friend will probably be happy to hear about it. You'll feel your relevance rise on the spot.

Keep an open mind while looking at the list. You may decide you'll have to participate in some type of activity you previously didn't take a shine to. In doing so, you will learn the key to relevance: relating to other people's sweet spots. Open yourself to something new, because there's a great chance you'll like it and wonder why you never did it before.

You might be surprised to learn that you don't know your frequent contacts as well as you thought, much less their passions. Don't despair. If you're drawing a blank, ask people to talk about their favorite hobbies, and encourage them to describe them. Give them space to talk, and really listen so you can understand why they enjoy what they do.

Your friends will appreciate your giving them a chance to discuss their passions, and you'll find that your relevance increases simply because you are showing an interest. Be willing to share some of your passions to kick-start the conversation. But remember, this exercise is not about you.

I suggested you start this conversation with your frequent contact circle. Once you're comfortable with it, make it a habit with others. Find out what people are interested in even before they fall into your frequent contact circle. If they want to show you one of their projects, take a look. You might find that no one has ever shown an interest in their passions before.

CONNECT NOW!

It's time to explore the three passions you circled in your journal.

Keep it real. Look for interests that truly resonate with you. Don't force yourself to enjoy knitting if it bores you to tears. If you have an aversion to magic, don't pretend you like it to conjure up a friendship. You will eventually be embarrassed when your insincerity becomes apparent.

Next, follow these four simple steps.

1. *Start a conversation with your contacts about their interests.* Talk about how appealing they are (if you truly think so) or how much you admire your contacts' passion about these things. They'll appreciate the fact that you even noticed.

I suggest this as a first step because you'll need to obtain permission to share the interest. Otherwise, some people might feel as though you're horning in on their hobby; others simply may prefer to do it alone. In this conversation, listen for details that might spark your interest and help you to sustain it; also listen for permission to keep talking about it.

2. *Participate.* If you receive permission to keep talking, you may be invited to join in. For example, a friend might invite you to go to the gym, a fund-raiser, or a game. Do it. Or be proactive and ask if you can participate even before you're asked.

Once you are there, give the event or activity a chance. Don't drag mental baggage along. Maybe you're off to the gym but have always seen yourself as a hopeless athlete. So what? Your friend probably doesn't care, or maybe you'll find out that your lack of aptitude is something else you share—except that your friend has decided to go ahead regardless. Don't let insecurities overwhelm possibilities.

3. *Add value to the activity you've just adopted.* Through research and keen observation, you may be able to find new ways that others can enjoy their passion even more. You may even get lucky and discover some new facet to a hobby that your frequent contact hasn't yet discovered.

Seminar attendee Kathleen, for example, learned that her friend Jim collected mounted quartz crystals when she saw dozens of them lined up in his office in a glass display. He explained that he'd been collecting them since he was a kid, and that he did so because he loved the beautiful formations and colors. Kathleen decided they were lovely too and started her own collection with Jim's help. Along the way she read a book about crystal healing and realized that the crystals may give off an energy that can help counteract the draining effects of fluorescent lights. When she shared this discovery with Jim, he was delighted. He found a whole new reason to buy more quartz crystals for his office, and it strengthened their connection.

4. *Be proactive.* Stay on the lookout for connections. As you talk to others, listen for their passions. Find opportunities to share in these mutual interests. Sometimes all it takes is a conversation. People take comfort in knowing that they are not alone in their interests.

Seminar attendee Bob told about the time when he and his lover, Tom, moved into a quiet rural town where they couldn't make friends with their only neighbor, an older woman named Sylvia. Bob and Tom would wave at Sylvia, take in her packages when she wasn't home, and even once gave her a ride to the store when her car wouldn't start. No matter—Sylvia remained aloof. Then one day Bob caught Sylvia crying on her front porch. She wasn't talkative but finally admitted that her cat, Minnie, had just died. Bob was a great cat lover himself; his own tabby had passed away only a few months before their move, and he helped Sylvia mourn the loss of Minnie. The two slowly became friends, and a few months later, when Bob took in a stray cat, Sylvia became her unofficial second parent. The cat now spends a great deal of her time at Sylvia's, as does Bob.

3. Connect with Others' Wants and Needs

The third and perhaps most powerful way to boost your relevance is to connect with other people's wants and needs.

You've already learned the importance of developing commonality. Now you will help provide something of value. By fulfilling others' wants and needs—be they for survival, sustenance, problem-solving, love, or respect—you can connect at the most basic level.

First, you need to assess what you can offer. What can you do for other people? What do you bring to a relationship or even a simple encounter?

Here's a simple exercise to do right this minute. Think of two areas in which you're really good at connecting with other people's wants and needs.

When I posed this challenge at a recent seminar, one attendee blurted out, "I've got a strong back to lift things that other people can't move. And I'm a great listener."

That's an excellent example of an impulse response. You'll think of your own. But come up with something, and you'll begin to uncover what's in your personal toolbox of helpful talents.

Now take out your L-factor journal and on a fresh sheet write "My Ten Solution Strengths." Think about recent occasions where you helped someone, or gave someone a boost, or inspired someone.

As a memory aid, analyze yourself from head to toe. What can you do? Are you a good problem-solver? Are you a source of information? Are you a great organizer? How about your hands— are you a natural-born helper, the kind of person who will do the necessary dirty work? Or maybe you're a powerful networker. You know many people, and you know how to connect them, fast. You might be surprised at all your helping capabilities.

When you're finished, review your list. These traits are the arrows in your quiver that make you highly relevant to others. Pull out this list from time to time to reassess your strengths and help yourself proactively build your relevance factor. (You'll also use this list in a future exercise.)

Now that you've made a primary assessment of what you have to offer, let's turn to other people. The ability to know what others dream about, or agonize over, is a form of intelligence possessed by the most relevant people in the world. After all, how can you solve a problem to which you're blind? Sensing others' needs is at the heart of developing a relationship.

The first thing you'll do is conduct a simple needs-and-wants analysis of your top contacts. Earlier, when you developed the top contacts list, you left two blank lines under each name. You've already filled one in with possible shared passions. Now fill the other line in with something this person needs or wants.

As a guide, think about what other people are required to do in life. Think about their dreams. Think about ways they like to feel, feedback they need to hear, projects they want to accomplish.

Maybe your friends need stress relief or assistance with a particular task. Maybe they want to feel respected, or maybe they need to have some fun. Find at least one want or need for each contact. Write it in the last empty line for each of your contacts. You now see ten opportunities to connect with someone.

Many seminar attendees find this exercise difficult because they've never stopped to think about other people in such a way. If this is true for you, don't feel bad. You just need to work on your ability to spot, recognize, and remember other people's dreams and requirements so you can connect with them in the future.

To do this, you'll want to develop an ongoing sensitivity to others. One of the best ways is to listen attentively when your friends speak. Be on the alert for words and phrases that signal their wants and needs. I call these *conversation key words*. They are cues that you've been given a great opportunity.

For example, when people use the words *need* and *want*, obviously you'll pay attention. Listen also for words or phrases such as *problem, challenge, crisis, overwhelmed, requirement, survival, or else, not enough, help, desperate, unhappy, miserable, demand, wish, hope, opportunity, desire, dream, responsibility,* and *duty.* All of these are golden nuggets to mine for a connection. Don't let them slip through your fingers.

If you don't feel you are hearing enough of these key words, speak up. One of the most effective questions you can ask is "Is there anything I can do to make your life better?"

One seminar attendee says his favorite wants-and-needs conversation starter is "What can I do to help you be successful?" Other questions people have shared with me include "What are you dreaming about these days?" and "What is at the top of your wish list?" and "What's keeping you up at night?"

When you observe people who are serial problem-solvers, you're probably seeing people who are masters of problem-prospecting. They can sense what people need, and they get involved.

The next step: Start connecting with others' wants and needs.

• *Pick someone from your top contacts list.* Look at the list again. You'll see your contacts' wants and needs. Then return to the previous exercise (My Ten Solution Strengths) and review what you have to offer. Find connections between what you can do and what someone needs.

• *Volunteer to help someone.* Raise your hand and offer your services as part of the solution. Be proactive. Say, "Can I help you?" to someone you know who could use the offer. Most people are quite glad to hear these words.

• *Don't make a fuss about what you've done.* Much as the staff at a great restaurant learns to be both excellent and invisible, fix things quietly. If you've done a good job, people will notice. You ruin the benefit if, after helping someone, you jump up and down drawing attention to your kindness. After a while, no one will think you're particularly kind.

• *Don't wait for the perfect time to act.* Whenever someone needs you is the perfect time. If you keep trying to pick the perfect moment to get involved, you never will.

Seminar attendee Scott shared the following story of a Johnny-on-the-spot emotional fix. One day he was walking to the elevator when he saw an acquaintance on her cell phone, complaining loudly. "That's it," she was saying. "I can't stand it. No one ever recognizes anything I'm good at."

Several wants-and-needs key words jumped right out at Scott, who also noticed the woman was wearing a floor-length pink cotton coat, just the kind Scott's wife would love but could never find. Scott walked up to the woman and said, "That's a great coat—my wife would shoot you for it. She's a pink freak."

The woman stopped grimacing. "Really?" she said. "I found it at the store across the street. I didn't know anyone else in the world liked pink as much as me. What's your wife's name?"

The two shared the elevator to the main floor, and by the time they were walking out the front door, the woman was in a great mood.

When Scott told a friend about the incident, she responded, "You took your life into your own hands. Can't you tell that's the wrong time to say something?" But Scott correctly guessed it was the perfect time. He gave the woman exactly what she needed, exactly when she needed it.

• *Remember to serve others' emotional needs, too.* In other words, try to help improve the way others feel. Here the out-of-pocket costs and time commitments are often small, but the psychological benefits can be huge. You don't want to get in the business of helping people raise money or move heavy furniture as a daily practice of relevance. But you can get into the business of raising moods and supporting feelings every day.

• *Exceed expectations.* Don't write a check that you can't cash. Don't tell others you're there for them, then disappear when they need you most. If you try to solve a problem you're not qualified to solve, you can come off as irrelevant

and unlikeable. Underpromise your solutions, and overde-
liver the results

No matter who you are, you can always add more to your
offer, boosting your relevance and L-factor. Here's how.

- *Keep adding to your personal résumé.* This is a list of all
your most important experiences, learning, skills, and assets—
at home, on the job, and in your social life.

To jog your memory to compile the résumé, take out two
items: first, the exercise from pages 168–169, in which you
assessed all you had to offer (My Ten Solution Strengths);
and second, your last employment résumé. Now, using the
latter as a guide, create your personal résumé. Just as every
few years your professional résumé changes, so too should
your personal résumé. Over time, add talents, abilities, and
experiences. Make sure that your personal résumé stays as
fresh and appealing as your professional one.

- *Try new roles in your personal and work life.* Learn new
skills by asking for and accepting new responsibilities.

Seminar attendee Adam, for example, decided to take over
the responsibility for dealing with contractors at home, including supervising appliance repairs and home-improvement
projects. Through this experience, Adam found a new way
to connect with the needs of several friends. "I never realized
how well I could do at hiring, managing, and motivating contractors," Adam said. "Once I learned how to manage contractors, I was able to help several friends through their home
repair crises."

- *Seek out and enlist a mentor to teach you something new.*
Look around for highly relevant people who seem to offer
solutions of great value. Ask them to coach you in these

skills. They'll probably be flattered and more than happy to show you what they know. Their insights can quickly add value to your personal résumé.

- *Teach yourself something new.* Spend time contemplating a skill you might like to learn. If you can't think of one, look at what others need, and learn a skill to help. Seminar attendee Lorraine noticed a dire shortage of piano players for her church's Sunday school services. She signed up for piano lessons, and within a surprisingly short time she was able to play for a youth group service. Lorraine's relevance at her church soared.

Don't overdo this advice, however. Focus on one thing at a time. If you possess the discipline to finish a single personal improvement project, you'll see more results than if you take on several at once and never master any of them. You can build relevance one victory at a time.

EMPATHY

1. Show an Interest in How Others Feel
2. Experience Others' Feelings
3. Respond to Others' Feelings

If you are truly empathetic, you'll understand other people's feelings and, at some level, will even experience those feelings yourself.

Of likeability's four components, empathetic skills may be the most difficult to improve. Some experts even feel that empathy is an inherent rather than a teachable ability, and that people either have it or they don't.

I disagree. I have seen many people work on their empathetic skills and better them. It may be hard work, but the results show it's possible. The following tips will help guide you.

1. Show an Interest in How Others Feel

Having another person show an interest in, and attempt to understand, our feelings is something we all crave and appreciate.

If you're not aware of others' feelings, you can be perceived as insensitive, either because of something you do (such as saying something inappropriate) or something you don't do (such as not responding to a call for help).

Understanding how other people feel is the result of a process that includes recognizing their emotions, listening thoughtfully, and then demonstrating your understanding by responding to their feelings.

The first step toward understanding how others feel is recognizing their emotions.

You can read emotions in others' faces long before they actually tell you how they feel. And whenever you spot a strong emotion, you're being alerted to a need for empathy. You're also being alerted to avoid insensitivity.

Dr. Paul Ekman, a professor of psychology at the University of California Medical School in San Francisco and the author of *Emotions Revealed,* has studied emotional expression for fifty years. Not surprisingly, he has found that a high percentage of emotional expression is found in the face. According to Dr. Ekman, "Facial expressions, even quickly passing, signal emotional expression. The face is the mind's involuntary messenger."

After conducting studies in dozens of cultures across the

globe, Dr. Ekman found that emotions are expressed consistently regardless of locale or custom. Different cultures may use varied auditory and verbal cues, but the facial expression of emotions is universal.

People convey seven types of emotion via the face: sadness, anger, disgust, fear, interest, surprise, and happiness. Dr. Ekman isolated three regions of the face that communicate all of these emotions: the forehead, the eyes, and the mouth.

Finally, he observed that most untrained people do not read emotional expressions accurately, which can create miscommunication and insensitivity. But with just a few hours of emotional expression training, almost anyone can double their effectiveness.

Based on Dr. Ekman's work and my own seminar experience, here are some hints on reading emotions.

- *Watch and study the face.* As you converse with others, make eye contact to center your vision on someone's entire face. You'll see activity in all three of the regions that send emotional signals. Look at the forehead—maybe it's crinkling; maybe the eyes are widening or the mouth smiling. If you're glancing at your computer, you won't see these signs.

- *Realize the emotions that are conveyed through facial expressions.* A frown signals sadness. The combination of a scrunched-up nose, lowered eyes, and a frown communicates disgust. Sound obvious? Then spend a day noting when you make some of these faces, and how few people seem to notice. (You'll find an example of each of the seven facial expressions and their matching emotions at www. timsanders.com/7faces.)

- *Pay special attention to quick changes in expression.* Dr. Ekman refers to these moments as "emotional leakage." People often allow their true emotions to slip out during un-guarded moments. After all, few of us can maintain a poker face forever. Eyes widen, then retract; lips curl or the noses twitch. Don't miss these subtle cues—they may be the only ones you receive. Remember, emotion is a mental state that triggers a physiological reaction, so the leakage can happen quickly and then disappear.

• *Use the media to practice your ability to visually detect emotions.* Newspapers, magazines, and television shows provide great content that you can use to sharpen your emotion-recognition skills. Pull out *Newsweek* or *People* and look at the pictures in a story, but don't read the captions. Guess the emotion first and see if you are correct.

One seminar attendee invented her own exercise by cutting out the pictures from a newspaper article. She then taped them to a blank page in her L-factor journal. Under each picture, she wrote down a one-word emotional caption. When she was finished, she read the original story and the captions beneath the photos, then tallied her results. By the sixth time she completed this exercise (using different pictures), her accuracy had doubled!

Another way to practice spotting emotions is to record a television program and watch the playback without sound. Note the emotions, then play the program with the sound on to see how well you did.

• *Notice all seven emotions, but especially watch for happiness.* When you recognize happiness, you avoid raining on someone's parade. People want to savor their positive emotions as much as they want to mitigate their negative ones. When you can read happiness, or even interest, in someone's face, you have an opportunity for a pleasant and easy empathetic conversation.

• *Don't jump to conclusions.* You may recognize an emotion such as fear, but that doesn't mean that you understand how the person specifically feels and the source of that emotion. To find out what's really going on, you'll need to have an empathetic conversation.

Dr. Ekman cites Shakespeare's play *Othello* as an example of the trouble caused by jumping to conclusions. "Othello murdered Desdemona because he presumed that emotions have only one cause," says Ekman. "Desdemona was afraid for her life because her insanely jealous husband had just killed someone who he thought was her lover. But Othello thought she was afraid because she was guilty of infidelity, so he killed her."

Don't be another Othello. Think before you leap.

Being a good listener is another excellent way to drive your L-factor higher. You'll need to listen thoughtfully, however, if you expect to understand how others feel.

• *Wear your listening cap.* In other words, always be ready to put yourself on mute mode, as you would a TV. How well can you be listening if you can't stop talking?

• *Don't interrupt.* Wait for an all-clear signal before you jump in to speak. Cutting people off, even if only to demonstrate excitement, ranges from insensitive to rude. In many cases, it will inhibit others from sharing their feelings.

In two-way radio communication, crossed conversations in which both parties talked at the same time used to be a problem. This conflict was resolved by implementing the simple system of saying "over" when one party was finished talking. During some Native American tribal council meetings, a talking stick is used as a device to conquer interruption; to speak, you must be holding the stick.

When you listen to someone, wait for the silent "over" signal, or to be handed the metaphorical talking stick, before speaking. It's usually a pause that says, "I'm finished, now it's your turn."

• *Provide a pregnant pause.* In other words, wait a few seconds before responding to what someone has said. Reporters, researchers, and psychologists frequently use the pregnant pause as a device to obtain deeper, more spontaneous information. A pregnant pause often makes your conversational partner rush to fill the silence with additional, generally unscripted, and frequently very revealing content. Allow even more time after you hear the "over" signal, and pay attention to what the other person fills the space with. Be sparing with pregnant pauses—too many can send the message that you aren't really paying attention, or that you're dreadfully slow to respond.

• *Think about what other people say and how they must feel.* Don't always ask yourself, "What does this mean for me?" Concentrate on the other person's feelings and keep yourself, your situation, and your feelings out of a listening conversation.

• *Ask, don't tell.* When you speak, ask questions about your conversational partner's feelings. Telling him or her what you think or what to do is not listening (unless he or she specifically asks). It will stop that person from sharing with you. Ask questions regarding feelings rather than facts. When you ask only about facts, you can sound like a detective; when you inquire about feelings, you're an empathetic supporter.

- *Pay attention to what* isn't *said.* Compare what you see to what you hear. Does the face match the words? If you spot a contradiction, let the face be your guide. Sometimes emotions are hidden behind fancy words but are obvious in the face. Learn to watch for conflicting signs, and become a master of interpretation.

- *Commit yourself to being a better listener.* Ask for help. Tell your closest friends you're trying to improve your listening skills. They'll give you feedback from your conversations with them as well as their observations of your conversations with others.

- *Test to see whether your instincts are correct by asking your conversational partners if you've heard them correctly.* You can guess—"That must make you feel very angry"—and you'll be corrected if wrong. Don't provide feedback with an air of authority, though. You're listening, not concluding. You can even ask for confirmation by saying, "Let me see if I get this straight. You're feeling angry because of this situation, right?" If you're wrong, don't despair. People appreciate your effort. Ask for the correct answer and for more information.

If you are able to master effective emotion-reading listening, you will dramatically boost your empathy factor. People will find your instincts sharp and your listening skills soothing and generous.

2. Experience Others' Feelings

When you listen to, and reflect back on, others' feelings, you raise your empathy factor. An even deeper level of empathy is achieved when you actually experience those feelings yourself; your connection moves from your head to your heart.

When you successfully understand and assume other people's emotional states, they can sense your authentic involvement. You can't fake this kind of connection.

Achieving this level of empathy will also help raise your L-factor because when you can see things from others' point of view, it will be easier to be friendly and relevant to them.

When a film character moves you, you cheer for him. He makes mistakes, he isn't perfect, but you forgive him. You may even end up crying for him, or laughing with him, and applauding when he succeeds. Real life can work the same way. When you feel another person's pain, you understand that pain through experience. It hurts. It's easier for you to develop a friendly attitude toward that person because you identify with her. You can see life through her eyes, and are more sensitive to her wants and needs.

Sometimes empathy comes naturally. At other times, when you attempt to experience how others feel, you feel a disconnect and draw a blank. Most people are inconsistent in their ability to adopt another person's perspective.

To boost your empathy factor, you need to sharpen your empathy skills. The secret lies in your imagination. Imagination is a kind of mental muscle, and you'll need to work it out to develop it. Here are some ways you can develop your empathetic imagination.

- *Accept other people's feelings as legitimate.* Don't judge or resist them. You may well question their facts or interpretations, but if you doubt the legitimacy of their feelings, you'll fail to find empathy for them. You're not trying to judge whether they're right. You're only trying to understand how they feel about a particular situation.

- *Try on a new point of view.* One way to approach this is to take on another perspective in bite-size chunks. Try some easy imagination exercises. If you know a friend's background, imagine you grew up in his or her neighborhood. Think of that area's influences, sights, and sounds. Then imagine why your friend must feel the way he or she does today. These mental pictures may fall short of keying you into this person's real feelings, but they may provide insight into his or her mind-set.

- *Flex your imagination.* Stretch it in ways you haven't tried before. For example, think of one person whose feelings you have recently identified with. Take out your journal and write his or her name. On the line underneath, write down the person's feelings. Was he or she feeling happiness? Sadness? Anger? On the next line, write "Because" and then a few words about the source of those feelings. Why did this person feel this way?

Now close your eyes and pretend you are in the person's shoes—literally—standing on his or her soles. Imagine yourself looking down at the tops of those shoes. The better you can create a visual image, the easier it will be to make the transfer. With your eyes closed, raise your head and say the feelings aloud. For example, "I feel sadness." Now say aloud the "because." For example, "I feel sadness because my best friend has moved across country," or "I feel anger because my boss lied to me." Take a few seconds and recall the details from your empathetic conversation. Remember everything— hopes, dreams, facial expressions, the extra information between the pregnant pauses. Be quiet for just a moment and reflect. Open your eyes. Can you feel anything?

• *Ask for details.* More information can help you successfully imagine how another person feels. If you can't make the necessary connection during a conversation, stop. Listen harder. Ask questions. Get the full story. But when you're collecting these details, remember that you're researching for feelings, not prying for facts. When you know more about the context of a feeling, it will be easier for your imagination to grasp it.

• *Walk a day in someone else's shoes.* Physicians treating overweight patients do just that in a program developed by the federal Centers for Obesity Research and Education (CORE). One of CORE's goals is to help doctors understand their patients' perspective by having them wear an oversize, weighted "empathy suit" to physically experience obesity. Donning the suit, the doctors spend an entire day looking and feeling extremely overweight. Participating doctors have found that others treat them very differently when they wear that suit.

What is the empathy-suit equivalent for your situation? Perhaps you can try on someone's day by performing one of his or her tasks. If someone tells you that he or she feels angry about having to do a menial job, do that job for a day and see what it feels like. (My old boss Jed at Der Wienerschnitzel was able to experience my feelings by doing this.)

Or ride shotgun—observe the experience at first hand. If a person fears a particular social situation, accompany him or her. Watch how events transpire and how he or she reacts. This exercise can help you feed your imagination with actual hands-on experience.

GET IN TOUCH WITH YOUR OWN EMOTIONS

You may still be coming up empty when you push the transport-and-imagine button. Perhaps this is because you lack awareness of your own emotions. The more you are aware of your feelings, the better you can identify with others'. In fact, many child psychologists argue that as we age, it becomes much easier for us to feel empathy because we have more life experience to draw upon. We know what other people are feeling because we've been there.

Here are two pieces of advice.

1. *Review and reflect on your feelings.* Awareness of your own feelings increases your ability to sense other people's feelings. Learn to reflect on how you've felt in the past so you can understand how other people feel today.

In your journal, write the header "My Feelings." For the purpose of this exercise you'll work on four emotions: sadness, anger, fear, and happiness. You may also want to come back to your journal weekly and write about some of your more memorable feelings and feelings you've observed in others.

For the moment, let's work on just one emotion. Underneath your header, write "Sadness." Think about a time you've felt sad. Write a one-sentence description of that feeling. On the next line write what caused you to feel that way. And on the third line, write three words to describe how you felt during that moment. You might use words like *loss, disappointment,* or *confusion.*

Now take a fresh piece of paper and repeat the exercise for anger, fear, and happiness.

Some of my seminar attendees have told me that in doing this exercise, they identified emotions they had never previously stopped to think about. Most important, many reported that the exercise later helped them imagine others' feelings by making them more aware of their own.

This is the real purpose of this exercise. Empathy is the experience of the other, not of you; you are getting in touch with your own emotions in order to strengthen your empathetic imagination.

2. *Build your imagination skills by observing empathy.* Research it. Many empathy training courses use movies as a device to demonstrate feelings, vivid results, and resolutions.

Dr. Bill Edwards of Columbus State University provides movie recommendations to students taking his interpersonal and small-group communications classes. Among them are *Children of a Lesser God, The Breakfast Club, Driving Miss Daisy, Groundhog Day, How Stella Got Her Groove Back, The Birdcage, The First Wives Club, Rain Man, One Flew Over the Cuckoo's Nest, Babe,* and *Terms of Endearment.* (Visit http://empathy.colstate.edu/films.htm for the complete list.) By watching these movies, you'll gather more reference points to feed your imagination.

Besides viewing movies, investigate other means of observing empathy. A range of entertainment options is available. One teacher of empathy, Stephen Covey, recommends reading fiction. He says that "if you read more stories of drama, coming of age, and other types of experiences, you'll be a more empathetic person because you will expand your emotional horizons."

A friend of mine says live theater works best for her, because she feels the emotions expressed by the actors in front of her. Still another friend thinks that television dramas are the best empathy teacher, because by watching these shows in her own home, she experiences an emotional intimacy that she feels is missing in public settings.

Experiencing the feelings of another person may come easily, or it may require much work. In either case, it is a proactive experience, something you must remember to do. Imagination and tenacity are required. You need to be willing to suspend judgment, assume new walks of life, and ask yourself tough questions to move from understanding feelings to feeling them yourself.

3. Respond to Others' Feelings

Most of the time empathy requires only the ability to understand how others feel. But if someone expects you to do something with this understanding, and you are unresponsive, he or she may doubt that you really do know what's going on inside.

There is a fine line, however, between empathy and intrusion. Make sure you really need to act, and that you'll truly add value by doing so. If you jump the gun and spring into motion every time others tell you how they feel, you'll be seen as too intense, and few will want to engage you in conversation. Most people prefer to air out their feelings rather than have someone act upon them.

There will also be moments when your responsiveness will make all the difference in your L-factor. The following are several tips on responding to someone's feelings to boost your empathy factor.

• *Remember conversations.* We live in an age of information overload. Most of your empathetic conversations occur with people you see often. In many cases, they'll want to pick up the conversation where they left off. If you've forgotten what you learned in the last conversation, you won't appear very empathetic.

One way to recall conversations is to immediately take a few minutes to reflect on them, with a special emphasis on the emotions involved and how they were expressed. You could also make entries in your L-factor journal to gather some of these thoughts. Not only does the act of writing commit thoughts to memory, the journal may come in handy the next time you talk.

• *Make yourself available for a follow-up conversation.* In a single conversation you usually just scratch the surface of a person's feelings. You may have discussed sadness, when deep down he was actually feeling fear. He himself may realize it later and want to talk with you again. After all, you're a good listener. Empathy is not a onetime affair. It's an ongoing process of listening, understanding, feeling, and listening again.

• *Share feelings.* At the end of a conversation, after you have listened thoughtfully, reciprocate and share details from your own emotional life. Consider divulging a secret, as Dr. Maguire did in *Good Will Hunting.* In so doing, you will build trust. Shared feelings can form a powerful bond; when you open up with your own private emotions, you may inspire someone to open up even further and engage in a deeper and more healing conversation with you.

As always, be careful. For instance, talking about your own happiness may take away from someone else's celebration and make you look self-serving; similarly, you don't want to compete with someone else's sorry state by complaining that you have it worse. But if you can make it clear that you've been in a similar place, your friend will feel less alone as he or she realizes that others can feel equally afraid, sad, or lonely.

• *Validate feelings.* As strange as it may sound, people often feel guilty for having feelings. Perhaps they believe that they don't deserve to possess their emotions, or that they're out of control, or that their bad feelings make them a bad person.

A surprising number of people confuse feelings with reality. If they feel they want to hurt someone else, they experience guilt, as if just thinking such a thought makes it happen. It doesn't. All of us have many feelings, good and bad, coursing through our brains all day.

When you let others know that you understand this, and that whatever feelings they're having are okay, you help them to realize that just having feelings is no crime. The guy who's so angry at his neighbor that he wants to kill him isn't a bad guy, as long as he deals with his feelings, recognizes where they come from, and gets past them. By letting him know that you understand why he feels so angry, you may help him conquer his anger.

- *Be a sponge.* Offer a shoulder for others to cry on. Sometimes people restrict their emotions to small facial expressions because they're afraid to let them out. Yet bottling up these feelings may be driving them crazy. As you improve your ability to recognize emotions in others, you will occasionally find that they need to air them. Your emotional availability may well provide others with the healing they so need to repair their hurt.

The young winner of a greeting-card company's contest to find the "most caring child in America" offers an excellent example of the effects of providing catharsis. One morning a child and his mother were observing their elderly neighbor sitting on his porch, upset. His wife of many years had passed away a few weeks earlier, and the man was feeling sad and alone. The child instinctively walked to the man's porch and crawled up on his lap. Later that afternoon the mother noticed the man was out of his chair, sweeping the porch and whistling. She asked her child, "Whatever did you say to him?" The child replied, "Nothing, Mom. I just helped him cry."

REALNESS

1. Be True to Yourself
2. Be True to Others
3. Share Your Realness

Are you real? This is the fourth question someone may ask about you after determining whether you're friendly, relevant, and empathetic. It will also be the fourteenth question they ask, as well as the fortieth and the four hundredth, because it will be a nagging, recurring theme in all your relationships.

If the answer to this question is no, your L-factor will plummet. Everything you've accomplished up to now will be severely discounted. But if the answer is yes, your L-factor will rise, and your other features will be enhanced.

1. Be True to Yourself

The very first question you'll have to answer requires you to look in the mirror and ask yourself: Who am I?

You must know the real you. If you're unaware of your identity and your values, you'll have a very difficult time staying on course.

In this section you'll complete three exercises to help determine the answer. Several seminar attendees, after finishing the exercises, reported that they could enunciate their values aloud for the first time; others were reminded of past values they'd forgotten about; and still others thought of issues that they needed to consider in the future.

Complete the following three exercises in your L-factor journal.

STATE YOUR MANIFESTO

A manifesto is a public declaration of principle or intentions. Here you will identify your key values by writing a statement about your strongest belief. It's similar to articulating a campaign promise, a mission, or a commandment that you insist other people meet when dealing with you.

To help you write your manifesto, answer as many of the following questions as you can (use a new page in your journal): What do you talk about when the conversation is about values? What was the last piece of advice you gave somebody that you felt strongly about? What do you stand for that separates you from the pack? If you give money to a cause, what kind of cause is it, and why do you make that contribution? Is there a recurring proverb or saying that you find yourself repeatedly spouting?

Take some time with this exercise. Some people find it difficult. Don't give up! Try to come up with at least one statement that describes something you feel strongly about.

On the other hand, if you come up with more than one idea, examine your answers and search for a recurring theme.

Seminar attendee Larry reported that "the last piece of advice I gave was 'Never minimize a youngster's accomplishment.' " Larry also said, "One of the things I define myself by is that I never make a child feel stupid." From this, Larry was able to craft a single-sentence manifesto: "Parents should first and foremost breed self-confidence in their children."

Another attendee knew exactly what she stood for and said so. "Self-esteem," she replied. "Even when it gets me in trouble. It took me most of my life to develop self-esteem. I like it in myself, and I like it in others."

One young man determined that his personal manifesto was "I believe in fairness for the little guy." He came up with this concept when he realized he'd recently signed a petition to keep a large discount store out of his neighborhood because he felt it had an unfair advantage over the local mom-and-pop grocery store. Also, the last organization he joined was a nonprofit group dedicated to helping small businesses.

Still another attendee went through pages and pages of notebook paper, scribbling idea after idea before seeing a pattern. "Everything is really about honesty," she realized. "I never knew it before, but I guess since all my notes are about how people should be truthful, and how much I love integrity, that's what I stand for."

Moving from your notes to the above questions, write a sentence or two that represents your personal manifesto. This is what you stand for. It's a statement you should never violate. If you did, your realness factor would drop like a stone.

IDENTIFY YOUR THIRTY-ONE FLAVORS

In this exercise, you're going to come up with thirty-one words that describe the real you. This exercise will sharpen your ability to enunciate exactly who you are and what you do, as well as the impression you make on others and how you are seen or see yourself.

Write "My 31 Flavors" on a new journal page. Then put down seven words that describe you day to day, such as *happy, forgetful,* or *anxious.*

Next write six words that describe you at your best. Then write another six words that describe you at your worst.

Now write six words that describe your role model, or any person you look up to. Finally, ask a friend to supply you with six words that he or she would use to describe you day to day.

On a single sheet of paper, you will now have thirty-one words that depict you from a variety of perspectives. This set will be fairly realistic, as you have portrayed yourself from many possible angles.

On another piece of paper, write the ten words from the list that you feel best state who you really are. Title this new list "My Frequent Flavors." These descriptions will serve as a reference for you later in this section.

CREATE YOUR OWN PERSONAL HISTORY CHART

Now you will create a graphic to represent you from birth to the present day.

Many organizations, companies, and even celebrities compile a history chart that describes their milestones, challenges, and best and worst times. You will create something similar to help you see your personal history on a single piece of paper.

First, make some biographical notes in your journal. Think of at least five significant events you experienced as a child, both accomplishments and failures. Next recall your life as a young adult, and select five more significant moments—perhaps meeting a friend who changed your life, starting your first major job, experiencing your first major failure, or passing a significant family milestone. Then identify at least five more milestones in your life. (For a long-form version of this exercise, read *Self Matters,* by Dr. Phil McGraw.)

Take out your journal, open it to a new page, and turn it sideways to make it wider than it is tall. (To use a computer-printer term, you are now looking at it in landscape layout.)

Write a *B* at the far left side of the page, halfway between the top and bottom. This stands for your birth. Write a *T* on the far right side of the page, halfway between the top and bottom. This stands for today. Now draw a horizontal line across the center of the page from left to right. This line demarcates positive and negative. You'll place the positive milestones above the line, and the negative ones below.

Now return to your milestones. From your list of at least fifteen, select the dozen most significant events, reduce each to a headline of a few words, and plot them according to when they happened in your life and whether they were positive or negative. If the event was very positive, write it high above the line. If it was very negative, place it well below the line.

Something that happened to you at age six would be close to the *B*. Last month's milestone would be close to the *T*.

(See the illustration on page 195 for an example of a finished personal history chart.)

If you don't get it right the first time, don't despair. Many seminar attendees made two or three attempts before they felt their chart was presentable. But when you're finished, you'll have a physical representation that can serve as a focal point for remembering your accomplishments and challenges.

Nearly all of my seminar attendees found the process of recollecting the ups and downs of their lives helpful for answering the question "Who are you?" And for almost everyone, it was the first time they had reduced the good, the bad, and the ugly to a single page.

| | |

The last three exercises have helped you draw a picture of the real you. You know what you value, you've identified some of your beliefs, and you've charted your personal history. Now that you know who you are and where you've been, embrace it. Be true to yourself. Be true to your roots, even if you are growing out from them. Remember your past—your friends will.

MY PERSONAL HISTORY

- Won spelling bee
- Honor roll
- State debate champ
- Won college championship
- Met Jacqueline
- Wrote book
- Started at dot-com company
- Hired at Yahoo!

- Moved, now poor
- Dad died
- Drinking problem
- 21
- Didn't finish college
- Changed jobs, was broke, _in debt_
- Took bad job that paid well
- Drinking/drug problem _depressed_

B ─────────── T

Here are seven additional tips for keeping true to the real you.

1. *Let your values be your compass as you navigate life.* Your beliefs and your actions should overlap. If you're contemplating an action that contradicts your manifesto, be careful. It probably isn't true to you.

Whenever you begin to question your current strategies, take out your journal and reread your personal manifesto. Does it support or conflict with your actions? When you feel internal conflict between what you're doing and what you believe, you're probably headed in the wrong direction.

2. *Spot-check your behavior for consistency with your values.* When you're considering a new personal strategy, meeting a new group of people, or going through an intense experience, take a few minutes and write down five words that describe you in that moment. How would you honestly describe your actions? If the five words from this spot check don't mesh with your thirty-one flavors, or if they violate your manifesto, you've slipped out of your true character. Ask yourself why. These spot checks will help you return to your true nature and, through repetition, improve your ability to see your unrealness as it unfolds.

3. *Practice seeing yourself from an outsider's point of view.* One way to do this is to imagine floating up to the ceiling to look down on yourself. See yourself through the eyes of someone who's observing, not judging or even interpreting.

In *The Power of Now,* spiritual guide Eckhart Tolle talks about "being the watcher." When you learn to be the watcher, you can monitor your actions as an impartial spectator rather than as an ego-involved participant. In this way you can witness your actions clearly and see them as others might. You can even see how others might judge you by them.

Another way to practice watching is with your tape recorder. Capture one of your conversations over the phone. (Again: Never violate your friends' privacy; tell them they are being recorded.) When you listen to the playback, don't think about your voice and how you sounded. Listen to your thoughts, your words, your tone.

Videotaping yourself is another way to become the watcher. Then you can look at your own personal reality show. Watch yourself as you would any television personality and make notes on who this person is; compare it with who you want to be.

4. *Borrow only with permission.* There is a fine line between being a student and being a thief. Throughout this chapter you've learned to observe other people who display friendliness, relevance, and empathy. When you admire others, it may be tempting to steal their catchphrases, mannerisms, or even personality traits outright. Don't. One of the earmarks of realness is that you are being you, not someone else.

Instead of copying, ask questions. Get feedback. Innovate. Integrate these new practices into your own routines.

5. *Protect your realness with self-confidence.* You may not be confident of all of your abilities, but that doesn't mean you shouldn't admire your true self. Invest time and effort in developing a level of respect for your real self, because it's the fortress that will protect your realness factor when you are challenged or afraid.

Revisit your personal manifesto. Ask yourself: If you met someone who possessed your manifesto, would you think highly of him or her? Chances are you would. You may lack self-confidence per se, but few people actually dislike their core belief system.

If you still can't develop enough confidence about the real you, return to the Finding Your Likeable Self exercise on pages 134–138. Look at those attributes again. Pay special attention to the likeable qualities you're most proud of. Read them aloud to reaffirm your personal value.

Seminar attendee Todd reported that he now carries a three-by-five card in his briefcase listing his manifesto, his favorite flavors, and the top two things he does that others like. Whenever he feels nervous, he reads the card to boost his confidence before he engages with other people. This helps remind him who he is and that he's a good person. It also stops him from becoming an unlikeable fake, because when he feels comfortable with who he is, he doesn't have to brag or tell white lies to make others like him.

6. *Discount the reasons you have for disliking yourself.* I'm not suggesting that you overlook your faults or ignore your mistakes. But there's a difference between accepting fault and engaging in self-loathing. You can like yourself even if you don't like the mistakes you've made. You may despise the situation you've put yourself into, but it shouldn't become an attack on the real you.

Similarly, you may not like your current physical or mental condition, but that doesn't mean you can't be comfortable with your essence as a human being.

Your manifesto and values represent your essence. Most of what you dislike about yourself is connected to the surface you, not to your true nature.

When you're feeling down on yourself, take a deep breath and then take out your journal. Look at your personal history chart. See how much you've grown, how much you've struggled, and how much you've accomplished.

Admit it: Down deep, you rock. Learn to take self-hatred and challenge it. Reduce its power, and remember that you're a good person. You bought this book because you knew you had a solid L-factor that could go even higher. You have a deep-seated belief that you can add value to the world, so discount anything that contradicts that concept.

7. *Periodically revisit the real you.* As you mature, improve, and become influenced by others, you will morph into a newer type of you, a version 2.0 or 3.0. Your manifesto as well as your values may change over time. You will develop new flavors and retire others. You will still be you, but a slightly wiser and older you.

Every year redo the exercises at the beginning of this section. Reaffirm your manifesto and values, as well as the thirty-one flavors that describe you this year. Start out with a new page, a new positive/negative line, and fresh points. Date the new chart and look at it one week later. Reflect on it. Ask yourself: What have I been through? What have I accomplished? What good luck have I enjoyed? What hard times did I survive? Such introspection can give you a fresh perspective that can increase your self-knowledge.

Look for gradual evolution, and be cautious of total revolution. Most personal change is incremental. If you see a stark contrast between this year and last, ask yourself if something so monumental happened that it morphed the real you. It can happen, but for the most part, this is where movies and real life diverge. People seldom change radically and quickly. Be proud of whatever positive changes you have made, and give yourself credit for them, no matter how small.

2. Be True to Others

When you establish a high level of realness with other people, you are as solid as a brick house. But each time others perceive that you are not being true, they mentally take a brick out of your foundation, and you become a little less sturdy in their eyes. Eventually, if they remove enough bricks, their perception of your realness crumbles.

Follow these seven techniques to ensure that your realness remains as solid as a brick house.

1. *Don't forget your past.* If you develop selective amnesia (remembering only what you want to while overlooking the rest), your realness factor plummets.

Perhaps you've conveniently forgotten your background. Maybe you're turning your back on your old friends and fans. As some people move on up in the world, they find it easy to forget those who've supported them in the past. This phenomenon is not limited to lottery winners or instant celebrities; it can happen to anyone. You move to a flashier city, get a better job, or reach a milestone in your life, then decide to lose your old crowd.

It's hard to get away with such an unpleasant attitude, however, as portrayed in the countless number of movies on the subject. Most recently, in *Sweet Home Alabama,* the lead character pretends her background is much fancier than it is; she is eventually exposed, as are most people who pretend they're something they're not. (This film has a happy ending; however, as noted, real life often differs from movies.)

When your life improves dramatically, remind yourself of your history, your friends, and your roots. Keep a copy of your personal history chart handy to help you remember your life's ups and downs. By acknowledging the link between today's successes and yesterday's experiences, you raise your realness factor with others.

2. *Share your glory.* Few of us are totally self-made successes. Almost everyone has had some help from a mentor, a sponsor, a teammate, a coach, or a friend.

Every time you experience success of any type, make an effort to share it with everyone who contributed.

To help you remember who supported you, take out your journal and write down the header "Recent Success Stories." For the next year—or as long as you choose—create a new listing whenever you achieve anything, from buying a new home to landing a promotion to earning some other form of recognition. On one line, write what happened, such as "Got a new job." Below it, explain how it happened.

For example, under "Got a new job," you might recollect that you heard about an opening at Fantastic Futures from your hairstylist. A friend then arranged the interview, while a previous employer offered a great reference letter. Retrace the steps and the people involved.

When you finish, circle the names of the people who made a difference. For each name you circled, ask yourself if the outcome would have been different had this person been absent from the story. If the answer is yes, he or she added value and deserves part of the credit.

Now ask yourself if you gave him or her that credit. If you didn't, do so. In the future, make a habit of sharing your successes with those who helped you. The response will be so positive, you'll enjoy the process even more.

Seminar attendee Joyce found that once she got in the habit

of sharing the credit, both at work and at home, she became addicted to the resulting appreciation. "It made me feel as good as my own success," she says.

3. *Practice humility.* Humility requires both self-awareness and self-discipline. When you overestimate your value, you experience false pride. False pride isn't pretty. People who have an inflated view of themselves and their accomplishments are generally perceived as out of touch with reality—and are usually disliked.

Remember that few of us are so great that we can lord it over others. Accept compliments graciously, but don't let them swell your head. Your head is probably just the right size as it is.

But don't go overboard and turn down compliments you truly deserve. If you are too humble, you could cross over into false modesty, and that is unreal.

You may ask, "But what if I really am great? Can't I say so?" One seminar attendee, Pranesh, put the best answer this way: "Goodness is good enough for others. That's all they expect from you. When you feed the perception that you are better than good, people will try to dress you down and prove you are not who you say you are. When they are successful at this—and they probably will be—they'll think you're a phony and eventually forget about all your positives."

Those with humility usually have a high L-factor, too, because they reinforce the belief that they are good but stop short of calling themselves great.

4. *Watch out for exaggeration.* It's easy to fall into the habit of adding a little length to each fish we catch. If you receive four calls after running an ad in the paper to sell your car, you are exaggerating when you claim that your phone is "ringing off the hook." It may seem harmless, but exaggeration is a habit that's easy to fall into. You get excited, and before you know it, you add a little color, a little weight, and a lot of oomph to your story. Each time you do this you decrease your perceived truthfulness, as well as people's perception of your realness.

Everyone exaggerates, but if you overdo it, others will eventually see you as a teller of tall tales, and everything you say may be called into question.

Remember that realness means factual and actual. Exaggeration is one of the most common ways in which people hurt their realness factor. Just calm it down and retain your L-factor.

5. *Learn to say, "I don't know."* No one likes a know-it-all, especially because no one does know it all. Yet too many of us are fond of pretending we know the answers even when we don't have a clue.

When you always claim to know the answer, people will think you have an unrealistic sense of yourself. In contrast, people who are honest about their lack of knowledge on a particular topic garner high realness factors from others. One of former television host Johnny Carson's most likeable traits was evident when he turned to a guest after hearing something new and exclaimed, "I did not know that!"

6. *Be honest when you make a promise.* If you tell someone you are going to do something, do it. If you decide you are not going to follow through, admit it. People will appreciate your honesty. People with a low realness factor are masters of promising great things but seldom execute. Though their lofty words may produce short-term optimism, their failure to deliver slowly erodes their credibility and their L-factor.

When you make a commitment, agree on a date or a time, and either make a note of it in your schedule or ask your friend to follow up with you. This proactive accountability will increase the perception that you are real and that others can take your promises to the bank.

7. *Recruit a reality coach.* Many times we lack the perspective to realize when we're being real and when we're falling into puffery. Pick someone you trust and make a deal. If he or she will be your reality coach and give you fast and honest feedback, you'll do the same in return. Give him or her permission to call you on an exaggeration, question the validity of your statements, and remind you of your past. This pact will provide you with a helpful set of eyes and ears and increase your ability to be truthful with others.

3. Share Your Realness

You've already learned how to be true to yourself and to others. But to elevate your realness factor, you'll need to produce memorable experiences of realness. You'll need to exceed expectations.

I discovered this phenomenon in 2003 while conducting an L-factor seminar in Seattle. I asked more than a hundred seminar attendees to select among everyone they'd ever known the one person they found the most real—their reality kings and queens.

Then I asked the audience to rank their realness royalty on a scale of one to ten. When I collected the answers, I threw out anything below an eight and was left with three dozen responses. I asked why these people had been scored so high. In two cases, consistency was the cause; in the other thirty-four, the audience members pointed to a specific, expectation-exceeding experience they'd had with that person.

I've done this survey a dozen times since, and the results remain the same—more than 90 percent of seminar attendees gave someone an ultrahigh realness factor because of one specific experience.

Seminar attendee Sarah described a meeting with her realness king, a local celebrity who she felt was completely engrossed in their conversation, making her feel as though she were the only person in the world. She also was impressed that he could be so down-to-earth as to have a casual conversation with her at a burger stand.

Another attendee, Elizabeth, recalled a ten-year-old conversation with her reality queen, who admitted to an annoying and destructive fault. That honesty was both endearing and revealing to Elizabeth. She remembered the conversation as if it had just happened.

These stories highlight just a few of the many ways you can share a moment of realness with others. In general, these techniques include being present; admitting that you are human; and being generous with your self, your emotions, and your feelings.

BE PRESENT

Whenever you are with others, be with them 100 percent. We live in a world of attention deficits, of pagers and cell phones and myriad distractions, where few people give others, or anything, their undivided attention.

Commit yourself to being with someone else. To achieve that level of presence:

- *Dedicate blocks of time for discussion.* Chance meetings can be filled with distractions. When someone wants to talk with you, set aside a specific time and mark it on your schedule.

Treat that time as a psychologist or an attorney treats a billable hour.

- *Turn off all interruption devices.* If you're in your office, set your phone on do-not-disturb mode, and switch off your computer monitor. If you're wearing a pager or carrying a cell phone, switch it to silent mode. If you forget and one of your devices rings during your conversation, don't answer unless it's an emergency, then turn it off and apologize for the interruption.

- *Ignore obvious distractions.* You won't always be able to talk with someone in a private location. You may be at a food court, a gym, or a mall. Block out all the surrounding distractions as though you were wearing blinders. Your level of concentration will send a powerful signal that you are present and listening.

- *Fend off any interruptions.* If a third party approaches, assert yourself. Explain that you're busy. Make it sound important. It may well be.

- *Maintain eye contact.* When you spend your time looking at everything and everyone except the people you're talking to, they'll get the sense you're not interested. When you look directly into their eyes throughout the conversation, they'll feel engaged.

- *Relax your body.* Tapping fingers and shifting feet say that you're not really there. Learn to take a deep breath, relax, and listen.

ADMIT YOUR MISTAKES

When you're big enough to confess that you made a mistake, you create a moment of honesty. These moments define you as someone who can be trusted to tell the truth, the whole truth, and nothing but the truth.

Every mistake you make provides you with a golden opportunity for a moment of honesty. Reinforce your realness by admitting guilt. Others already know it's your fault, and your honesty will be music to their ears. They will savor the feeling that you trust them enough to tell it like it really is. Such moments defined many seminar attendees' examples of the most real person they know.

When sharing a moment of honesty, you must:

- *Admit to yourself you are wrong.* You've already learned how to play the impartial third party and honestly assess your actions. Now let the watcher tell you when you're wrong. Stop trying to make excuses for yourself. Relax and admit it.

- *Don't delay your admission of guilt.* Putting it off for months or years will make your moment of honesty seem weak or even insulting. The longer you let it simmer, the more likely the other person is to be boiling over when you finally speak. While there is no statute of limitations for personal mistakes, the fresh ones are the best ones for an honesty moment.

- *Have a face-to-face conversation.* Sending an e-mail or a note is a poor way to communicate your admission, and it seldom creates a moment of honesty. It's true that in a live conversation, you run the risk of being confronted by others. They may ask you why you erred, and you'll have to answer then and there, and that can be scary. Be big enough to look other people in the eye, or listen to them as they tell you the impact of your error. You'll survive.

- *Provide details.* It isn't enough to admit what you did. Explain why you did it. The other person wants to know what you were thinking at the time, what led you there—and when you realized you were wrong. These topics are all important, and you should be willing to address them. No one likes to hear "I don't know" in such conversations; it sounds as though you're avoiding the real issue.

- *Explore remedies.* When you admit fault, you open the door to solutions. Ask other people what they think you should do. Be open-minded about their suggestions. Don't rush to accept the first plan of action they put forward, or reject it out of hand. Think it through. You want to avoid future errors with this person. If you overpromise and under-deliver, you will negate your moment of honesty.

- *Be willing to correct yourself when you are wrong.* Just because a well-run newspaper runs corrections doesn't mean it loses all credibility. If you make an assertion that you later learn was wrong, admit it. Seek out those you misinformed and tell them. If possible, discover the correct answer and provide it instead.

This practice will also deter you from offering knee-jerk, incomplete answers. It's no fun constantly correcting yourself, so the more you're willing to do it, the more vigilant you'll become about your assertions.

BE GENEROUS WITH YOURSELF

Let the true you come out to play, and let others share your passions, fears, emotions, beliefs, and vulnerabilities.

Perhaps you've been taught to hold back such thoughts and

feelings. Perhaps you want to blend in to avoid embarrassment and to prevent others from obtaining information that could be used against you someday.

Instead, learn to take smart chances and savor those moments of personal sharing. When you share a small piece of yourself with others, you increase your realness factor because people get to experience your true nature.

Share your emotions. Seminar attendee Chaz told a story about the most real person he ever met—Tom, the CEO of the large manufacturing company where Chaz worked. Tom was holding a difficult meeting during which he announced that due to an economic downturn, he was laying off a large portion of the workforce.

Although Tom was a macho type, he couldn't hide his sadness for the families who would be affected. As he spoke, tears streamed down his cheeks. Chaz saw his boss as a sincere man who had no choice, even though Chaz himself was let go in the downsizing.

Share your beliefs. When the time is right, discuss a conviction about which you feel strongly but that you may never have mentioned. This belief may be social, political, or spiritual. But be smart. It's real to let people know a little about your values, but it's not wise to try to convert them. Share your beliefs when appropriate with trusted confidants. Never wield them like an ax.

Share your dreams. Talk about what you long for. Don't be embarrassed to express your aspirations. Perhaps by sharing, you'll be more likely to achieve that dream.

Share your fears. If you're afraid of a particular situation, confide in someone. The ability to admit fear drives up your realness factor by showing your vulnerable side. As always, be intelligent about picking the right person with whom to share your fears.

Don't worry if sharing doesn't always work out as planned. In truth, it doesn't always work. And sure, you run a risk in being generous with yourself. People may take advantage of you from time to time. They might even laugh at you. But these instances will probably be rare, if you are smart about selecting your confidants. By and large, your generosity with your deepest, truest self is a gift, and most people will respond by admiring your realness—and raising your L-factor.

Afterword

oday we live in a world where L-factors aren't nearly as high as they could be. People don't yet realize that likeability is the key to success, both personal and professional, and few of us practice likeability as a part of our daily routines.

We know all too well what the world looks like today. But what would it resemble if it were filled with high L-factor people? Consider these scenarios of life in a more likeable time.

A twelve-year-old girl moves from a rural town in Missouri to metropolitan Chicago; her father has landed a job in the city and is relocating the family just before the new school year.

On the first day of class, the girl boards the school bus; there the driver welcomes her by extending his hand to help her enter, and a little boy scoots over in his seat to make room for her. When the girl arrives at school, another helpful student shows her to her homeroom class, where she checks in with her teacher, who opens the class by introducing the young girl to everyone else. Even though the new girl's clothes aren't sophisticated, you wouldn't know it by the other students' reactions. They smile at her openly and greet her pleasantly, and the girl feels very welcome. A half-dozen kids clamor for the opportunity to show her to her next class. As she walks down the hallway, a smiling vice-principal gently pats her on the shoulder and asks her how she's feeling.

At the school cafeteria, several classmates join her for lunch. They talk with her about music, boys, and movies. She finds out that although these kids' interests and hobbies differ from those of her old friends, everyone is open to listening to her opinions.

At the end of the day, she leaves school and sees her mother waiting for her patiently in the parking lot. "How was your day?" she asks. The girl smiles and tells her it was just great.

| | |

A customer-service agent is having a tough time at Los Angeles International Airport. So far, three flights have been canceled and more than thirty bags have been lost—all before lunch. This is the last business day before a holiday weekend, and the weather isn't cooperating with flight schedules. The airlines are also feeling the residual effects of a work stoppage, which has impacted the quality of baggage handling. The line of distressed customers is thirty deep and filled with impatient business travelers as well as anxious parents with crying babies in their arms.

Yet not a person is yelling, screaming, or issuing veiled death threats to the agent. Instead, the agent experiences an orderly and reasonable assortment of human beings. One by one the customers calmly explain their grievances. In some cases the agent can provide a remedy. In others she cannot. The people she can help thank her profusely and wish her a great day. The ones she can't help are disappointed but reasonable—they too wish her a great day. Certainly many of the more distressed travelers are upset at the inconvenience, but they are quick to point out that their frustration is not aimed at her.

In the break room at lunch, the agent chats with her coworkers about the morning's events. The day has been demanding for everyone, but no one is dejected or overly stressed. They all agree on one thing: Although this is a hectic business, they feel lucky to have a job where they get to talk to people all day.

| | |

A cabdriver in Atlanta rolls into traffic first thing on a Monday morning. Rush hour is in full swing, and it seems as though more cars than ever are lining the roads. Road construction is jamming a major freeway exchange, and several accidents are causing the freeways and surface streets to resemble parking lots. Everything is moving in slow motion except the clocks and watches. It is also hot and muggy, even though it's not yet 9 a.m.

Despite it all, few horns are blaring, and even fewer drivers are shaking their fists at one another. Instead, the cabbie witnesses a calm scene. Drivers politely negotiate with one another calmly and quickly, like ants marching off to work.

The cabbie picks up a fare at a downtown hotel and crawls through the traffic jam toward a northern suburb. The customer is late for her meeting, but she doesn't demand that the driver step on it. Instead, since she knows there's nothing he can do, she relaxes and tries to enjoy herself. The driver asks permission to turn on the radio; the passenger consents. Eventually she arrives at her location, a little sweaty from the ride, but in good enough spirits to give the driver a handsome tip. He thanks her and picks up a new fare on his way back into the city. This new passenger knows that traffic is at a standstill and asks the driver simply to do his best.

| | |

A twenty-seven-year-old freelance journalist is attending his first Internal Revenue Service audit. He's understandably nervous, even though he doesn't think he's done anything wrong. The previous night he tossed and turned in bed. Now, on the morning of the audit, his next-door neighbor helps him prepare by reviewing tax law with him, advising honesty and openness.

When the young man arrives at the IRS office, a cheerful receptionist points him to a chair in the lobby and fetches the agent. A few minutes later a friendly woman with a clipboard and a file calls him by first name and introduces herself as the agent responsible for his audit. She motions for him to follow her down the hall, where she parks him in a conference room and returns with two cups of coffee. She notices that he is visibly distraught, so she spends the first few minutes of the meeting calming his jitters. Through conversation, they soon discover they both grew up in New Hampshire. They converse and laugh at each other's my-hometown-is-smaller-than-yours anecdotes. The writer eventually relaxes, and the audit is conducted.

Unfortunately, there are a few problems with the filing, and the agent does not allow some of the man's write-offs. But although he has misfiled and owes some back taxes, the agent doesn't make him feel stupid or dishonest. She assures the young man that many people make these mistakes and that he has no reason to be ashamed. At the end of the meeting, the agent thanks the man for his honesty and gives him her card for any follow-up questions or concerns. The writer shakes the agent's hand and thanks her for her sensitivity.

As he leaves the office, the receptionist tells him to have a nice day, and the young man wishes her the same. Just another typical day at the IRS.

| | |

An exhausted mother of three is finishing her workaday marathon of chores and activities. She got the kids fed and off to school, spent a few hours cleaning the house, and went grocery shopping. In the afternoon she did homework for a community college course she is taking. Then she made the kids an after-school snack and helped them get started on their own homework. Next up on her agenda: preparing the family dinner.

Now, as she is washing the dishes, her husband comes into the kitchen and sits down at the table to do some office paperwork. He immediately notices the frustration in her face. He puts down his files and asks her what's on her mind.

At first she says nothing is wrong, but with some gentle prodding she opens up and admits how unhappy she feels. The husband becomes engrossed in her description of her week, and how low she's been feeling over the last few months. She feels overworked, underappreciated, and lonely. Her husband's new business seems more important to him than the family.

When his cell phone rings in the middle of the conversation, the husband turns it off without breaking eye contact. And after his wife finishes venting, he confesses that given all the time he is spending at work, he is partially to blame for her problems. He offers to help her improve her work-life balance, then promises to contribute more to their home life, even if it means hiring someone else at the office to cover for him.

Before she falls asleep, the wife thanks her husband. She remembers their first date—how attentive he was to her every need and how connected she felt to him. She's glad he's still the same man, or perhaps even better.

| | |

An unbelievable world, you say? Impossible? Unrealistic? I don't agree. This world could be ours, if we were to all become likeable.

But the transformation is unlikely to happen if you don't do your part. It's up to you to stop unlikeability dead in its tracks. It's up to you to raise your L-factor—if not for yourself, then for all the people with whom you come into contact. Your shining example could inspire and ignite a movement of high L-factor behavior throughout your sphere of influence.

Not long ago I flew to Chicago to give a seminar on likeability. Because my flight was early, I found myself with a few hours to pass on a beautiful spring day, so I took a walk around the city.

On a side street off Michigan Avenue, I noticed a quaint brick preschool, tucked away behind several larger buildings. Through its freshly washed windows, I noticed a brightly colored poster emblazoned with the question HAVE YOU MADE SOMEONE SMILE TODAY?

Anyone who has a high L-factor can answer that question with a resounding "Yes!"

Like the children in that Chicago preschool, we were once told that if we put a smile on someone's face, we'd grow up to be healthy, wealthy, and wise. Somehow between childhood and adulthood, we lost our way. We've forgotten our duty to make others smile. What happened to that seven-year-old who gave out Valentine's Day cards by the box? At thirty-seven, you're probably lucky if you send just one.

Even if you once were lost, now you are found. You now know how to raise your L-factor. This newfound knowledge was never meant to live only in your head; it was meant to be shared. Make it a part of your personality; make it a part of your life. Challenge and stretch yourself to be more likeable. To quote the words of Kilgore Trout, Kurt Vonnegut's alter ego, in Vonnegut's novel *Timequake*, "You were sick, but now you're well, and there's work to do!"

Tonight, before you fall asleep, ask yourself, "Have I made someone smile today?" If your answer is no, make sure that tomorrow night the answer is yes. The rest of the world is depending on you.

Acknowledgments

An army of wonderful people helped me deliver this book to you. There isn't space to name all of them, but I particularly want to give thanks from the bottom of my heart to:

Billye Coffman, my mom. She taught me so many of the lessons and values I've drawn from in writing this book.

Jan Miller, my literary agent. Thanks also to Kym, Shannon, and the rest of the staff at Miller-Dupree for having faith in this idea, as well as for making room for me in your star-studded stable.

Annik La Farge, my editor and advocate at Crown. Also, thanks to the rest of the Crown gang, including Steve Ross, Doug Jones, and Darlene Faster.

Don Weisberg and Madeline McIntosh at Random House, my friends and my random rooting section.

Heidi Krupp, my publicist, as well as Chris, Laura, and the rest of the staff at Krupp Kommunications, for keeping my profile public.

Ryan Mills, my research director. He put in countless hours researching, fact-checking, and agonizing over this book. You rock.

Robert Shindell, George Kao, Anne Woodward, Jim Seymour, Macaire Merkel, and Shelly Boss, my beta testers.

Dr. Stephen Covey, Dale Carnegie, Daniel Goleman, and Eckhard Tolle, who wrote such wonderful books that they inspired me to try my own.

And finally Gene Stone, my writing partner and mentor. Gene, you've demonstrated grace, mad skills, and a commitment to the reader's experience. You are the key to this book.

About the Author

Tim Sanders is the author of *Love Is the Killer App: How to Win Business and Influence Friends,* a *New York Times* bestselling book. He lives with his wife and son in northern California, where he serves as the leadership coach for Yahoo!